MW00928314

Warrior Women
Prepare for battle

Author: Andrea Kellum
Cover Artist: Sylvia Spielman
Photographer: Leah Savage

You are brave!

Copyright © 2018 Andrea Kellum, Changing Crowns Ministries

All rights reserved.

ISBN: **9781983033032**

Dedication

Lovingly dedicated to my beloved husband, Jeremy Kellum, who has shown me grace, patience, and love from the first day we met, who taught me how to study God's Word in a way that caused me to fall in love with the scriptures, and who has proven a million times over, through his actions, what Christ-like love should be.

And to our precious son, Kainen Kellum, who has listened to me read this book more times than we can possibly count, who reminds me daily of the miracles Jesus still performs, and who gives me the best hugs on my worst days.

You both have helped to strengthen me in becoming a mighty Warrior Woman!

Acknowledgements

My sincerest appreciation, gratitude, love and prayers to my dear friend, Sylvia Spielman, for your unselfish gift of sharing your artwork with others. May God bless you with opportunities to continue to serve Him and may His face shine upon you all your days.

To Leah Savage, my strong, mighty, and beautiful sister; you have proven yourself to be a warrior woman for Christ in more ways than one. Thank you for using your talent of photography to help me share what God has called me to do in this book. I pray your life is overflowing with favor.

To my parents, Adrian & Kim Farley; all my siblings, Wade & Kayla Farley, Christian & Amber Crowe, Drayton & Emily Farley; my nephew, Axton; my grandmother, Mimi (Ruth Burns); my family-in-love, Terry & Patty Long, and Robert & Shirley Cook, all of you have worked endlessly to encourage me through every trial and battle I had to face to complete God's message. May God restore all the enemy has destroyed, and may He bring you an abundance of life, joy, peace, and love.

To Pastor Wayne Keeton, Sister Dianne Keeton, and all our church family at The Refreshing Place Church, thank you for your support, love, blessings and opportunities to serve our Savior along side each of you. You truly will never know the multitude of ways God has used you to help me grow in my walk with Christ. I pray your gifts, encouragement, and love is given back to you ten-fold.

To my sweet and mighty Warrior Sisters of Coffee and Jesus, words will never express how much joy each of you have brought to my life and how much you keep me moving forward on days I want to simple hang my head in defeat. You have each allowed me to flourish in God's purpose for my life. May He forever remind you: You are worthy! You are enough! You are beautiful!

To my best friend, Brandy; I don't have enough time, space, or words to tell you what a blessing you are in my life. You have dried my tears, made me giggle, spoke to me with firm and purposeful love, kicked me into action when I needed it, and let me be 100% of who God created me to be, 100% of the time, without judgement. You truly are one of my strongest warrior sisters. I pray the Lord allows you to walk in wealthy places, restores your loses, blesses you with wisdom, and pours favor over you and every generation belonging to you forever and ever. I love you beyond words, my sweet Bun.

Meet the Cover Artist

Sylvia Spielman is the artist behind the book cover for Warrior Women. Andrea and Sylvia attended a woman's bible study lead by Sylvia in Fall 2017, where they had an immediate connection. As Andrea began to tell Sylvia about her new book and how God spoke to her about it, Sylvia quickly recognized the title. It was the same as a painting God had given to her in a dream years before. Throughout this book you will also see other images of the entire painting she created. Sylvia's story is shared below.

"In the spring of 2013 I dreamed several times of completing a very large painting. In the dream the colors were rich and intense which indicated to me the medium would be oils on canvas. I saw three women clothed in rich purple and bright blue on a background of golden wheat. Each time I woke, the words of Isaiah 41 were on my lips .... You will be a new threshing instrument with many sharp teeth. You will tear your enemies apart, making chaff of mountains. You will toss them into the air, and the wind will blow them all away; a whirlwind will scatter them. Then you will rejoice in the Lord. You will glory in the Holy One of Israel. (Verses 15 & 16) I knew it was an image placed in my heart to convey a message. As women we must be stronger than we think. Not in anger as the world would dictate, but in stamina and determination. The enemy wants our marriages, our children, our communities and our dignity. It is with concerted prayer and faithfulness we must fight. God's promise is that He will hold us up in battle; He will scatter those who stand against us. Let the Warrior Women of God stand together in unity for those we love." - Sylvia Spielman

Sylvia has served as Secretary for New Life Assembly of God @ Woodstock since July 2007. A graduate of University of Montevallo, Alabama she completed two BA programs: Family Consumer Sciences and Visual Art. Her education and work experience have provided exposure to the social and life development of all ages. Her music ministry of 35 years has opened many doors of opportunity to serve in local women's ministry through music and speaking. Her personal hobbies include art and home improvement. Sylvia's four sons are grown and married. She has nine grandchildren.

About the Author

Andrea Kellum is the founder of Changing Crowns Ministries, a former internationally recognized pageant coach, national pageant titleholder, worship leader, author, speaker, and homeschool mom. She has been married for 15 years to Jeremy Kellum and they reside in Woodstock, Alabama, along with their teenage son, Kainen.

Andrea passionately serves women in her community and around the world as a teacher of WAR night at The Refreshing Place Church and as the founder of Coffee and Jesus; a live daily devotional group for more than 4,000 women from every state in America and over 33 countries worldwide.

Her desire is to help women better understand God's word, to encourage them to find their identity in Christ and to love women in Christ-like ways that bond all Christian women in a unified, and strongly knit together community. Andrea hopes to use her ministry in a manner that teaches women to embrace every intricate part of their individual purpose in Christ.

Contents

Introduction

Throughout my life I have been placed in situations that have allowed me to grow in my personal walk with Christ. I have gained skills that developed into resources to expand God's kingdom. However, I was never fully aware of the defined purpose of those moments until about Spring 2017. My life began to play out a series of events that caused me to once again come to the place of choosing paths. At this time, I would also find myself in circumstances that caused me to have an overwhelming need to find where God was leading me. As I worked through challenges I knew were presented to strengthen me, I had a sense of awareness and a desire to share God's word with the world full of women He created. Each time I learned something new I couldn't wait to tell the next woman I saw all about it. Days and weeks went by and I discovered more and more of this new road God was walking me down. Then, as if I should have known all along I was consumed with a notion to begin sharing devotions and writings of God's messages; and later in this book you will read about that moment in great detail. During this time my mind became flooded with words. Sometimes so random I thought to myself, "What is wrong with you? What does that one word have to do with anything in your life? Is there purpose in what is happening? Ok, God, is this really you?"

The words kept coming in like a telegram delivery system, all day, every day. I wrote each one in a separate note on my phone; giving each word its own place to flourish, hoping soon I would have the answers to why these words were individually important and urgent. I knew they each held a message. I knew they would each become a lesson, a devotion, a teaching I would eventually share with the women in my life.

However, on one particular day, as I sat studying, praying, fasting, reading every biblically based book I could find, and watching every women's ministry seminar on the internet, two words poured into my thoughts in a way they could not be ignored.

Warrior Women!

I wrote them on a note on my phone and stared at them. Then, in an indescribable, instantaneous way I had this knowledge…

"Andrea, keep these words quiet. They are special. They are not to be share as a devotion. These two words will become a book when the time is right."

What just happened? A book? OK, I've written a book before, a pageant guide for my clients, and I love writing, but really, Lord, a book?

Never did I have a reason to anticipate that as God was shaping and molding me, as He was teaching me to fall deeply in love with His Word, never did I have the slightest thought that I would one day write a book.

And yet, here we are, you and I, ready to embrace this journey together. You are now holding the book God placed on my heart to write and share with women of all shapes, sizes, color, races, and denominations. The book God spoke to life and confirmed in ways that can only be explained by God's wondrous performance and timing. The book that I know God will place in the hands of millions, actually billions, of women, to strengthen, encourage, and prepare for battle against the enemy. You are special sister, God is trusting you on a journey that will stretch your faith, redirect your focus, and plant your feet firmly in the ground of the battlefield. And when you are prepared, when you have been equipped and fully armored for battle, you will not only fight with a knowledge of victory, but you will help teach and train other women, just like you, to stand firm, to guard themselves against attacks, and to declare victory in Jesus Christ against any power of darkness.

You are on to brink of becoming a powerful and mighty Warrior Woman!

"For God has not given us a spirit of fearfulness, but one of power, love and sound judgment." 2 Timothy 1:7 HCSB

Chapter 1

Prepare for Battle

I recall the words "prepare for battle" playing over and over in my mind. I didn't understand at all what they meant.

What battle?

How do I prepare?

What could God possibly mean by this?

A few months before this thought arose I had started noticing a change in myself. I was longing for, craving for, if you will, God's attention. I could sense the desire to search for Him becoming more profound and more in-depth dwelling in my spirit continually. I wanted more of Him. I wanted to know Him the way I saw others know Him. I longed to understand the difference between seeking Him and genuinely having a relationship with Him. I gave my life to Christ when I was a young wife and mom, only three months shy of turning twenty-one. I loved the Lord, and I knew Him already, but at this moment, I needed more of His presence. The desire was growing stronger by the day and looking back I don't think I even understood the fullness of what I was praying.

Jeremy and I, (by the way, Jeremy is my husband, and I may talk of him often in this book because he is a massive part of my everyday walk with Christ), had watched a new Christian film about prayer. I immediately came home, ripped out one side of my small walk-in closet, put up a curtain, added a small table, a seat, and a notebook and started my private prayer room.

I sat in that small place praying day after day and asking God to unveil His secrets to me. "What is your plan for me, Lord?", I'd cry out. And as I waited for my answer, patiently seeking His will, I heard this..

Silence.

Wait, so did I do this all wrong? I poured out my heart, wrote down my prayers and requests, and earnestly sought-after God's wisdom. Then where did I make a mistake? Did God not hear me? Did He not want me to know His plan?

Little did I know this was the beginning of a journey that I would be terrified of, but one that God would allow me to walk so that I would be prepared entirely for battle! I remember feeling so engulfed in fear that I began to memorize and repeat the same scripture night after night, and day after day.

"For God has not given us a spirit of fearfulness, but one of power, love and sound judgment." 2 Timothy 1:7 HCSB

I found a cute photo with this scripture on it, printed it out onto paper and tacked it to the wall of my prayer room. Every day that I walked in to pray I had to look at that scripture. I was reminded of it each time I walked in to pray, but I had no idea the importance it would have later in this new journey God was leading me on. At night, I would lie in bed repetitively quoting that scripture to myself until I would eventually drift off to sleep. This ritual would become a familiar moment to me as I began to learn what God meant when He said, "Prepare for battle!"

A little history...

Growing up I loved being a girl; everything about being a girl was fascinating to me. I loved makeup, dresses, princesses, and pretending to be a mom. I could go on listing for days the things I loved about being a girl. Then at the age of five, I competed in my first pageant, our school pageant.

That afternoon I had fallen asleep, and I remember being grouchy as my mom got me ready, which was odd considering I usually enjoyed getting to play dress up. My hair was curled, and light makeup was applied. I slipped into a beautiful yellow dress full of ruffles, and we proceeded to my elementary school. I don't have a memory of much more, but I do know I didn't place in the queen's court nor did I win the crown. It hurt my feelings so much that the next year I refused to be part of the pageant. This part especially humors me because I would later in life become so passionate about pageantry and working in the industry for the goodness and glorification of Jesus Christ, that even my family and friends thought I was crazy!

Throughout my school years, I competed in pageants off and on, winning or placing in most occasions, but there were a few times I merely accepted the participation trophy with a smile. I look back now at these times, and I know they were experiences God gave me to better help my clients in my adult years. Yes, you better believe it, I grew up, married my sweetheart, had our only child, (a miracle story in itself), became a dental assistant, then a hair and makeup artist, then a work from home mom, and finally a full-time pageant coach.

God lead my path in pageantry from having local hometown clients to becoming an internationally recognized pageant coach with clients all over the globe. He placed within me a strong, passionate desire to be a light for Christ in an industry that desperately needed it. My journey in pageantry lead me to many opportunities to serve our Lord and teach others about Jesus Christ. Eventually however, God would tell me this part of my ministry was over as He prepared me for battle as a warrior woman!

Battle Plan #1
Recognize your battle

At the end of each chapter, you will find a battle plan page, like this one, designed and intended for your warrior woman writings.

These ten pages are purposefully created to get down into the depths of your heart, the place where you may not typically go, to help you become better equipped for your battle.

Do not take these pages lightly! The enemy is armed and ready to attack, and we must be armed and prepared to fight back and conquer. The battle is real!

Before you can begin preparing your armor, you must recognize your struggles and begin to learn your story better than anyone else. In pageantry, there is a saying "be yourself." Now, it's meant to encourage contestants to be who they are and not worry about trying to be who they think the judges want them to be, but I had a different saying for my clients. Don't just be yourself, know yourself!

If the enemy is going to take his time to study you and watch you and recognize your strengths and weaknesses, then, girlfriend you better know them too!

1. What is your battle? I didn't quite recognize my battle, nor did I have knowledge that I was even in a battle. You are also in a battle most likely. If you don't feel you are facing a current struggle, then think of a past struggle. You may even be facing multiple battles. Grab a notebook and begin to write down your battles. Recognize them! Be truthful and honest!

2. Find a scripture or scriptures that will help get you through your battle as we prepare. When I was consumed with fear, I clung to 2 Timothy 1:7! Praise God for His word! Find your scripture and be ready to recite it often!

3. Your past can sometimes play a big part in who you are or what you're battling. Do you see a connection between the past and present in your struggles? If so, what are those connections and how is God using them to strengthen you?

"...He turned around in the crowd and said, "Who touched My robes?"'
Mark 5:30 HCSB

Chapter 2

The Unknown

Have you ever traveled to a new city alone? You aren't sure where the safe places are, or what restaurants have the best ratings. It can be a bit overwhelming tackling a big, new city by yourself. I traveled a lot within the last few years of my pageant business and one place pageantry always led me was to Orlando, Florida. Now, this is supposed to hold one of the happiest places on earth, but my friend, believe me, I was far from comfortable traveling there. This "raised in the country with no traffic light in sight" southern gal was trembling at the thought of my first 10-hour trip from home in Alabama to the grand city of Orlando all alone. I had been there before, twice actually, with Jeremy as my driver, but this first time alone was a bit more intimidating. It was filled with the unknown. However, I knew it was something I had to endure. I couldn't back out on my clients who needed and expected me to be there, and to arrive right on time as scheduled. I had no other choice than to face the unknown, head to head!

The next part of God's plan for me would look much the same. I would begin to experience physical things that no one could explain to me. It started early in the year. I would feel tired quite often. Not the tired you feel when you exercise, more like the tired you feel when you've exercised for a week. My muscles cramped, my joints ached, my head was foggy, and I forgot everything! By the looks of things, you would have thought that this next sentence would be me telling you I found out I was pregnant; but I didn't. In fact, I didn't find out anything! I was experiencing something so unknown to me and what seemed strange to everyone else as well, that even my doctor couldn't give me a definite answer.

When my symptoms first began I tossed each one off to the side. My dry eyes I blamed on my contacts, as I also blamed for my vision problems, and my eyes being sensitive to light. My hands and feet began to peel, and my skin was going crazy on me, varying between severely dry to itchy and hives. Then the joint aches started a few weeks later, and boy was that painful! I thought I had the flu. The symptoms were all there: low-grade fever, joint pain, fatigue, chills. Yep, seemed like the flu to me, but it didn't go away. As a matter of fact, it lingered, and even more symptoms arose in the following weeks.

I finally told my sister I wasn't feeling well and hadn't been for some time, so she forced me to the doctor; literally, she got the phone and called for me and then made sure Jeremy knew so he could take me. This probably shows a little of my stubbornness, but this walk is all about me being open and vulnerable.

Before my first visit, I did what any sick female would do; I researched the internet! Oh, how horrible a decision! I had scared myself into having every known disease to humanity! When I arrived at my first appointment, I knew my doctor would test for several things based on my research and symptoms. He did. What would happen next would be the beginning of a journey I knew God purposefully designed for this very moment. I couldn't have known this story of my life would be part of a book, but I did know that whatever unknown I was about to face had a mighty goal of glorifying Jesus Christ! Just like my first trip to Orlando, I knew this too was something I had to face, head to head!

After multiple doctor visits and tests, and I mean a LOT of tests, the conclusion came to this: fibromyalgia, dysautonomia, and ADHD. Hmm... Not the diagnosis I expected. I was of course given a series of medications; some worked, some didn't. I had good days, and I had terrible days. I had moments of joy and moments of depression. It started taking a significant toll on me mentally and somewhere in this part of the medical mystery I began to lose all hope! I began to feel helpless, crazy, pointless.

All the very things I had spent all those years teaching my clients about being confident I now felt were lies. I was filled with fear! I felt so much fear that I would cry almost entirely all day. There was even a point I remember Kainen (our son) coming to me and saying, "Mom, I'll be glad when you feel better"! How could this happen to me? I was always the person who was positive, uplifting others, joyful and so full of hope! I was the one who looked at others and cheered them on when they felt worthless and lifeless! I was an encourager, and I couldn't even manage to get out of this self-pity trench I had placed myself in, all the while knowing God had a purpose for this! Was the purpose for me to lie in bed day in and day out with fear and hopelessness?

I prayed! I prayed, and I prayed, and I prayed! Sometimes I would just sit and ask, "Father, Why? What did I do to deserve this? How can I help anyone when all I see is pain and fear for my life?"

I had lost my joy! I had lost my hope! I had lost my faith! Here was a battle that had me feeling defeated! I couldn't handle the constant depression, anxiety, stress, worry, fear, feeling that everyone thought I was crazy! It was too dark of a place for me, and I couldn't take anymore! Not one single second more of it! Something had to give! I needed a break! "Father, I am crying out to you to save me, and you are leaving me all alone!"

"But my precious child," I heard him say, "I haven't left you! You have left me. When did you read your bible last? When is the last time you sat with me in silence, not asking for anything but to rest in my presence? When did you stop singing for me and worshipping me with music?"

The humiliation I felt at that moment is indescribable! Here I was so consumed with ME that I didn't see that it was ME who turned away!

I've never had an experience like the one I am going to write about next. I had walked away, and God had made that very clear to me. So, I knew what I had to do next, and that was to turn around and walk back towards Him! As I was sitting in our living room one evening, I began to read the bible. I turned to Mark; no reasoning behind why it is simply where I started. I was seeking Jesus, so I began to read only the words in red. And that lead me to a moment with Christ I will never forget!

Mark 5:24-34 Tells a story of a woman who was diseased by a blood disorder. She spent 12 years searching for a cure, for healing. She visited with doctor after doctor, and no one could help her. She spent everything she had. Then she gathered into the large crowd that was following Jesus and reached to touch His robe. Scripture tells us that Jesus felt the power go out from Him and

"...He turned around in the crowd and said, "Who touched My robes?""
Mark 5:30 HCSB

This woman, who probably lived a very secluded or at least a non-social life due to the laws mentioned in Leviticus 15:25-27, found herself desperately seeking after Jesus. She knew if she could get to Him somehow and touch Him she would be healed.

As I read these scriptures in the book of Mark, it was as if Jesus Christ were sitting next to me on my sofa speaking these very words to me! Me, who had poured all I had searching for an answer for my illness, who had reached out to every doctor I could find to find a solution to my health problems, Jesus spoke to me! My eyes filled with tears and my heart was overwhelmed! I couldn't stop crying. Jeremy and Kainen were sitting with me distracted by something, not paying attention to me and then they noticed. As I tried to compose myself to speak and tell them why I was so overly emotional, I knew this moment was one of transitional breakthrough!

Reading the words of Jesus,
"Daughter, He said to her, your faith has made you well..." Mark 5:34,
was the crucial turning point in this journey of walking towards God's plan for me. I had been refilled, rekindled, a flame burned inside my spirit again! I knew God was telling me to worship Him once again in song! I was healed! I no longer was going to live in fear of what my body was doing. I would live in blessing and abundance of knowledge of what Christ was doing! So, I began to sing... In the bathroom, because we all sound prettier in the bathroom, right? I sang song after song, day after day. I read God's Word and felt it come alive more than ever before! He had restored things for me that I didn't think would ever be restored!

Sister, I want to tell you that Jesus is real! He is alive and real! His word is the truth! Christ is the way! The only way! And all He is asking is that we accept with the faithfulness of a child because we are His! Just like the lady with the blood disorder, we must have faith to find our healings, and hope to believe in Christ's power to make us warriors for God's kingdom!

I don't know what you are battling as you read this. I may not personally understand why you are worrying, but I do know that we have a risen King, a mighty Savior and there is Power in His name!

Today He is calling you to let go of what yesterday has shown you. Remove the enemy's lies from your mind, for we know that John 8:44 tells us the enemy is the father of lies. Begin to hear the voice of God louder than all others and prepare yourself for the next few chapters to become a Warrior Woman.

You are about to be armed and equipped with everything you will need to secure the victory in the battle.

Battle Plan #2
Facing Your Unknown

Part of my battle was fear of not knowing. Not all battles are the same, however. Your battle may be obvious and in-your-face, or you may be in a battle that you have now recognized but are afraid of standing on the front line to fight. I know what you feel like in all these situations. I believe before we can begin to attack, we need to wear armor, and before we can wear the proper armor, we must create a mindset of victory. You see, victory has already happened, Jesus Christ did that for us. But our battles will allow us to remind the enemy that we know, and we belong to The Victor. I challenge you now to change your thinking. Begin to see your battle in a new way, a fierce way, a victorious way! Answer these next questions with a Warrior's mentality. If we are going to become Warrior Women, we must look like a warrior, speak like a warrior, act like a warrior and THINK like a warrior.

1.   What is your greatest fear in facing your battle head to head? Recognize this fear, begin to find the root of this fear, and acknowledge the truth in it all.

2.   Do some research. Is there a story in the bible that speaks to your current battle or fear? For me, I connected instantly to the lady with the blood disorder. It's amazing when we open God's Word and find familiar people like us. I believe it gives us a more realistic understanding of what is happening in our own lives and then Jesus can transform everything.

3.   Music is my favorite way to worship. Its where I feel I can completely release my prayers, thoughts, and heart to the Lord. I want you to find a song or a few songs and create a playlist that you will begin to listen to before each day of study in this book. Let this be the time

you allow God to remove any distractions from your mind and allow the Holy Spirit to take the lead in where God wants to move you in fighting your battle.

One of the three ladies featured on Sylvia's painting titled,

"Warrior Women"

Each of the three ladies on the painting has a specific task, yet they are all brought together for the same unified purpose. This is exactly how I imagine each of us Warrior Women to become. Individually working our missions, but united for the same purpose of serving Jesus, gathering other women to join us, and being the light of Christ to women worldwide.

"Put on the full armor of God so that you can stand against the tactics of the Devil."

Ephesians 6:11 HCSB

Chapter 3

The Belt of Truth

Before a soldier becomes a soldier of war they must be trained, equipped and armored with proper attire. Consider this with me for a moment. Can you imagine a doctor trying to perform surgery but never receiving the proper training or tools? Or what about someone aspiring to be a chef walking into a kitchen to create a feast for many to partake but they don't have the recipe? It would be hard for both the doctor and the chef to be successful at what they are trying to accomplish.

Our journey to becoming warrior women is much the same. We must be properly equipped, adequately trained, and know the precise ingredients that when combined will create the most potent warrior woman we could ever imagine being!

Guess what? God gave us the secret formula! It's in Ephesians 6!

Let's look at the scriptures in Ephesians 6 and learn about our first piece of armor: the belt of truth.

"Finally, be strengthened by the Lord and by His vast strength. Put on the full armor of God so that you can stand against the tactics of the Devil. For our battle is not against flesh and blood, but against the rulers, against the authorities, against the world powers of this darkness, against the spiritual forces of evil in the heavens. This is why you must take up the full armor of God, so that you may be able to resist in the evil day, and having prepared everything, to take your stand. Stand, therefore, with truth like a belt around your waist, righteousness like armor on your chest, and your feet sandaled with readiness for the gospel of peace. In every situation take the shield of faith, and with it, you will be able to extinguish all the flaming arrows of the evil one. Take the helmet of salvation, and the sword of the Spirit, which is God's word. Pray at all

times in the Spirit with every prayer and request, and stay alert in this with all perseverance and intercession for all the saints."
Ephesians 6:10-18 HCSB

Verse 10 begins with "be strengthened by the Lord."
I don't know about you, but I'd be willing to say that like me you probably try to rely on your own strength most of the time.
It's a battle I face daily. I'm a problem solver! I want to help everyone create a world of good! I want everyone to be happy and get along! If there's a problem, there's always a solution, and I'm the gal who wants to find it! However, I'm beginning to learn that trusting and relying on God, the process of increasing my faith, means that I must allow His strength to be my strength. I can't always fix everything or everyone. No matter how much I try (or you try) we will never be capable of being independent of God, and we shouldn't want to be.

Paul reminds us of this in the next few verses. He teaches that we must put on the full armor of God and that we must be ready for battle against the enemy! Remember me telling you in chapter one how God was telling me to prepare for battle? Well, that's exactly what we are about to embark on, a journey of preparation.
1 Peter 5:8 tells us to be alert because the enemy is prowling around ready to devour us! If the devil is prepared and waiting to devour us at any moment, then shouldn't we be prepared and ready to fight our battles?

In Ephesians 6 we also see that our battles aren't with flesh and blood but with spiritual forces of evil. I find myself needing to be reminded of this often in my fights. I get overwhelmed or caught up in what is happening in a physical sense that I forget who or what I am battling is spiritual. We must stay alert and aware at these times, knowing that God has given us specific instruction to be prepared, to know how to fight and to understand how to battle as a warrior.

I love that Paul starts off with the belt. For a Roman soldier, that belt was crucial. The belt was the glue so to speak that held together the rest of the uniform. On a Roman soldier's belt, you would find a buckle, much like what we would see today, you'd see these metallic straps hanging from the front of the belt for protection, and the belt would also have a sheath for the sword or dagger of the soldier. The most important part about the belt is that it held the remaining gear together like the breastplate. Without the belt, the soldier would lose his armor and would be defenseless.

The significance of this being the first piece of armor we are told about is outstanding! It serves considerable importance in the battle. Our belt of truth is the truth of God's word, The Holy Bible.

Just like a Roman soldier must have a belt surrounding him to fulfill his warrior role, we must also be surrounded by the truth of God's word. This means we need to read God's word, memorize God's word and be ready and equipped to use God's word in our battles.

Let's look at what God says about learning, memorizing and speaking His word. Go with me to the book of Joshua chapter 1, and we will begin in verse 6.

"6. Be strong and courageous, for you will distribute the land I swore to their fathers to give them as an inheritance. 7. Above all, be strong and very courageous to carefully observe the whole instruction My servant Moses commanded you. Do not turn from it to the right or the left, so that you will have success wherever you go. 8. This book of instruction must not depart from your mouth; you are to recite it day and night so that you may carefully observe everything written in it. For then you will prosper and succeed in whatever you do. 9. Haven't I commanded you: be strong and courageous? Do not be afraid or discouraged, for the Lord your God is with you wherever you go."
Joshua 1:6-9 HCSB

When God called upon Joshua after the death of Moses, He spoke words of encouragement to Joshua. Within this set of scriptures our Almighty, Powerful God spoke a command to Joshua again and again. The command given was, *"Be strong and courageous."*

So often I have read these scriptures and applied them to my situations; Especially in times of doubt. But what I have obviously overlooked sits perfectly situated within these words from God.

Look at verses 7-8.
How many times do we hear verse 9 and overlook the rest?
God didn't only command Joshua to be strong and courageous; He gave him the exact formula for success that he would need to follow the command. It's right in the center of the obvious!

God told Joshua to

"...carefully observe the whole instruction My servant Moses commanded you. Do not turn from it to the right or the left, so that you will have success wherever you go. This book of instruction must not depart from your mouth; you are to recite it day and night so that you may carefully observe everything written in it. For then you will prosper and succeed in whatever you do." Joshua 1:7-8 HCSB
For Joshua to know God's commands sent through His servant Moses, for him to understand how to remain strong and courageous, and for him to follow God's promises to His people, Joshua must recite God's word, carefully observe it, not turn to the right or the left from it and THEN he will prosper and succeed.

Just like Joshua, we too will be ready to have victory in our battles when we follow the same protocol. Do you hear the voice of your commander, our Almighty God? Prepare your belt for battle and let's search for the next piece of armor!

Battle Plan #3
Knowing God's Truth

Along my personal journey of preparing for battle I had to learn to also keep my face in God's truth! I've always read my bible, studied with other women, had family and private devotion time, but I knew this particular journey was different. If God was going to prepare me to be a real Warrior Woman, one who could stand her ground on the battlefield, then I had to first know His truth and know it as fully as possible. This third battle plan is one that will take time, years even to finish. It is a battle plan that you should never actually end. Knowing God's truth is going to take time, dedication, wisdom, and prayer. You better believe that if anyone is cheering you on for this battle plan to work, it is me! Even if we never meet or I never know who you are, I can promise you, I have prayed for you over this matter and I am cheering loudly that you are so successful in this battle plan that the enemy runs and hides the moment your eyes open! I pray your knowledge in God's word and truth increase to depths that mere human words cannot express! I pray God blesses you with wisdom of His truth so strong and so discerning that even you become flabbergasted at God's work! This is the time to dig your heels in deep, sister.

1. Set aside a 30 minute to 1-hour time frame in your day for alone time with God in His word and in prayer. Don't tell me you don't have time. Wake up earlier, go to bed later, skip that dinner with friends, give up your favorite evening television show. You do whatever it takes to find time to plant your face in God's Word and to fall before His throne in prayer and thanksgiving. Write down your committed time in your notebook and stay committed to learning Every. Day. Of. The. Week.

2. Get a study bible. Buy yourself an easy to understand study bible and read as much as possible on each topic you study. If you don't know

where to begin, find your local Christian bookstore and ask an associate to help you or ask your pastor, husband, sister in Christ what they use and recommend. I can't tell you what having a study bible does for me when I study a topic from God. Having a better understanding of His Word is only going to ensure you are that much more prepared when the enemy strikes.

3. Find a Christian mentor and find someone you can be a mentor to. Hold each other accountable to memorizing scripture together. You can choose one chapter, one verse, one book. Allow yourself time to not just quote these verses but to understand the purpose in the original context and how you can apply it in your life.

Our cover woman! Isn't she fierce? When I was first brought into Sylvia's office, my eyes were immediately drawn to this Warrior Woman. I love purple, it is the color of royalty. However, I saw something intimidating about her. She reminds me of who I want to become; a fierce, unstoppable, woman on a Jesus mission. She represents royalty, strength, and leadership to me. Those are all qualities we can call ourselves in the truth of Christ!

"Lord, I turn to You."
Psalm 25:1

Chapter 4

Breastplate of Righteousness

Every time. Every single time.

As you begin seeking God with all your heart, you better believe that the enemy is going to start his deceitful tactics.

Whew! The voice of the enemy will get so loud in your head, and he will tell you lie after lie after lie!

It is easy to feel overwhelmed by all the voices we hear daily. With so many voices coming at us, it sometimes becomes hard to recognize God's voice verses the voice of the enemy. It's crucial that we understand how to take time to acknowledge and accept God's voice. The enemy wants us to hear his untruth, his lies, and deceit. But the Holy Spirit, The Voice of Truth is much stronger if we first learn to listen and accept it! God wants to lead us into the gracious and loving plan He has designed. God's voice will never lead us astray. The Voice of truth will always lead you to Jesus not away from Jesus.

Somewhere, in the midst of finding your armor to prepare for battle you'll most likely experience moments of defeat.

I want to share this scripture with you that God showed me in the center of being overwhelmed by troubles and trials and attacks of the enemy.

It's the scripture that allows me to pour out my heart to The Lord!

Psalm 25
"Lord, I turn to You. My God, I trust in You. Do not let me be disgraced, do not let my enemies gloat over me. No one who waits for You will be disgraced; those who act treacherously without cause will be disgraced. Make Your ways known to me, Lord; teach me Your paths. Guide me in Your truth and teach me, for You are the God of my salvation; I wait for You all day long. Remember, Lord, Your compassion, and Your faithful love, for they have existed from antiquity. Do not remember the sins of my

youth or my acts of rebellion; in keeping with Your faithful love, remember me because of Your goodness, Lord. The Lord is good and upright; therefore He shows sinners the way. He leads the humble in what is right and teaches them His way. All the Lord's ways show faithful love and truth to those who keep His covenant and decrees. Because of Your name, Yahweh, forgive my sin, for it is great. Who is the man who fears the Lord? He will show him the way he should choose. He will live a good life, and his descendants will inherit the land. The secret counsel of the Lord is for those who fear Him, and He reveals His covenant with them. My eyes are always on the Lord, for He will pull my feet out of the net. Turn to me and be gracious to me, for I am alone and afflicted. The distresses of my heart increase; bring me out of my sufferings. Consider my affliction and trouble, and take away all my sins. Consider my enemies; they are numerous, and they hate me violently. Guard me and deliver me; do not let me be put to shame, for I take refuge in You. May integrity and what is right watch over me, for I wait for You. God, redeem Israel, from all its distresses."
Psalms 25:1-22 HCSB

Honey, keep putting on your armor!
Grab it, quickly!

Our next piece of armor we will prepare is the breastplate of righteousness.

It's crucial for us to examine the literal use of the breastplate to understand the importance of this piece of armor in a spiritual battle. For a Roman soldier, the breastplate protected the most vital organs. The breastplate was made from metal, mostly iron, but often for wealthier soldiers it would be made from bronze. The metal would be overlapping layers that allowed the room for flexibility while in motion. It guarded the heart of the soldier against the enemy's sword!

The breastplate of righteousness, as well as the other pieces of armor, are not and cannot be created by us. They are battle gear given to us and created for us by God. Once we know this, we will begin to see that the righteousness needed in this piece is not our own and it can only come from our loving Father.

Look in scripture with me for a moment.

"He saved us — not by works of righteousness that we had done, but according to His mercy — through the washing of regeneration and renewal by the Holy Spirit."
Titus 3:5 HCSB

He saved us. Christ saved us. Nothing we do or did can save us. It's evident in Titus 3:5 that we are incapable of working to earn righteousness.

The righteousness of God is a gift. It belongs only to those who accept Jesus Christ.

It's essential for us to reflect on what Christ has done so that the threats and attacks of the enemy trying to accuse and blame us for being unrighteous will be quickly shut down.

I remember when I started feeling better and profoundly searching for God. The first few attacks I experienced were hardcore.

And the first weapon the enemy used against me was my past! He brought up every sin I had ever committed before knowing Jesus, and he even threw reminders of a few sins I committed after knowing Jesus. If ever there was a sign to me that I was on the right path this was it! The enemy using my past to attack what I knew was already covered and won by Christ only fueled my desire to search for God's plan more fervently than ever in prayer and fasting!

I may get repetitive with this, but God's word tells us that the enemy comes to kill steal and destroy. (John 10:10)

However, we know that Jesus came to give us life and life abundantly! Freedom from our sins, life everlasting with our Lord and Savior in eternity! We can live free because of Christ!

Let's walk the "Romans Road" scriptures together.

"as it is written: There is no one righteous, not even one."
Romans 3:10 HCSB

We understand that none of us are righteous or have the capacity to be righteous on our own.

"For all have sinned and fall short of the glory of God."
Romans 3:23

We all have sin. We are born from sin and into sin.

"But God proves His own love for us in that while we were still sinners, Christ died for us!"
Romans 5:8 HCSB

It is because of God's love for us that the sacrifice of Jesus Christ was accomplished!

"For the wages of sin is death, but the gift of God is eternal life in Christ Jesus our Lord."
Romans 6:23 HCSB

Jesus could have easily walked away from this sacrifice, but He knew the only way we would ever be free from the guilt of our sins and blameless before God was for death to be paid. His death was our gift.

"If you confess with your mouth, "Jesus is Lord," and believe in your heart that God raised Him from the dead, you will be saved. One believes with the heart, resulting in righteousness, and one confesses with the mouth, resulting in salvation."
Romans 10:9-10 HCSB

We are saved by confessing with our mouth that Jesus is Lord and believing with our hearts that God raised Him from the dead.

Believers know Jesus by faith. Our believing with our hearts is what results in righteousness.

How incredible is it, that when we simply believe and confess, God sees us covered by Jesus' sacrifice?

The breastplate of righteousness is only available for us to put on when we have accepted Jesus as our Lord!

Now, I want also to add that although we receive this gift, it is not a free ticket to continue in our old ways.

It is quite the opposite.

God's word tells us that the old is gone and a new person is established.

(2 Corinthians 5:17)

When we truly desire the truth and righteousness of God, we also begin to seek after His desires, His heart, His plans.

And because of this, our actions result in being obedient to God's commands.

Christ teaches us to follow Him. He tells us time and again that we are like branches which should produce good and plentiful fruit. It is because of our actions in following him that we will produce good fruit, the fruit of the spirit. (Galatians 5:22)

It is not our self-righteousness that we arm ourselves in battle with, rather it is the knowledge and acceptance of the righteousness of Christ that covers us.

That is the breastplate of righteousness!

Our hearts and our minds can be protected only by the true and pure righteousness of God.

Is your breastplate ready for battle?

Put it on.

Take a deep breath.

Now exhale.

Doesn't it feel great to be covered by the righteousness of Christ and know the weight of our armor is actually on Him?

Battle Plan #4
Hearing the Voice of Truth

This is the place the enemy will begin to use your past to try and defeat you. You need to remain focused, Warrior! Know who you are in Christ and that He has you fully covered!

1. Has the enemy already attacked you with guilt of your past? You may feel like what you did and how you lived before knowing Christ is too terrible to be completely forgiven. You are wrong and that is the voice of the enemy. Write in your notebook what guilt you are continuing to hold on to. Recognize the enemy's lies.

2. The only way you are going to defeat the enemy and begin to recognize God's voice and truth, is to know it. Begin to memorize the Romans Road scriptures this week. Print them out on paper, write them down, highlight them in your bible and place them all over your home, workplace, car and anywhere you will see them.

3. You are only as strong as your knowledge of the covering you have in Jesus Christ. On your own time this week begin to plant your face in the scriptures of Jesus' sacrifice. Study them fiercely and pray without ceasing that God will open your eyes to the vastness of His goodness and love for you! Warrior Sister, you are loved beyond human comprehension!

"...and your feet sandaled with readiness for the gospel of peace."
Ephesians 6:15

<u>Chapter 5</u>

Sandals of Readiness

Sandals of readiness: Standing firm in God's truth.

One of the first lessons I would teach my pageant clients was how to build confidence.

The instructions I gave them were simple:

    1.   Find three things you like about yourself; it can be a physical feature, a gift, a talent, anything that encourages and reminds you of how special you are.

    2.   Write those three things on a piece of paper and place it on your mirror.

    3.   Speak it out loud every day; facing the mirror, looking yourself straight in the eye, say what you wrote with all the confidence you can muster up inside of you. Even if you don't believe it say it again and again, louder and louder until you do!

With every new client, I would see change upon them doing this. A change didn't happen because of anything I did; it was because the truth they spoke about themselves became so embedded in their minds that the insecurities of other areas in their lives were overshadowed by the confidence they now knew as fact. It's a spectacular thing to watch when we speak positive, affirming, truth over and over.

Keep this in mind for the next few paragraphs as we move along in preparation. I promise to show you the reasoning behind me sharing this with you.

When I think of sandals, the first thing that comes to my mind is cute summer-ready shoes. Maybe gold with tassels that would look ever so cute with a long, flowing summer dress. You know like the ones you see in all the boutique ads on social media.

I'd like to say that's what we were going to talk about here, but this lesson on sandals will be far from the next viral fashion blog post.

The sandals of a Roman soldier were built for endurance and with great purpose!

More specifically these sandals are called *caligae*, (sounds like Cali-Guy). *Caligae* were made from layers of leather, laced up the center of the foot, sometimes to the mid-calf, and had iron hobnails on the bottom for reinforcement and to help with traction. These shoe spikes were similar to what we know of in the sporting world as cleats, and their purpose was much the same as well.

During a sporting event like football, softball, baseball, or soccer, cleats are worn to provide a steady foot so that the player can stay standing in the game. The same was true for a Roman soldier; they needed to remain standing. A soldier on the ground was not the best place in a battle, and these sandals were designed to keep them standing firm.

Sound familiar? "Standing firm."

Let's go back to Ephesians 6 again and see how many times standing firm is mentioned.

"Finally, be strengthened by the Lord and by His vast strength. Put on the full armor of God so that you can STAND against the tactics of the Devil. For our battle is not against flesh and blood, but against the rulers, against the authorities, against the world powers of this darkness, against the spiritual forces of evil in the heavens. This is why you must take up the full armor of God, so that you may be able to resist in the evil day, and having prepared everything, to take your STAND.

STAND, therefore, with truth like a belt around your waist, righteousness like armor on your chest, and your feet sandaled with readiness for the gospel of peace.

Ephesians 6:10-15

Three times we are told to stand. When in battle a soldier needs good footing. For the soldier to be as fully ready to fight as possible, he or she needs to be in an upright standing position.

Just as a football player needs to have security while playing on a potentially slippery field, a soldier needs sandals that allow a firm grip in the ground to stand against the attacks he will face from the enemy.

We are instructed to wear the sandals of readiness for the gospel of peace; Sandals of readiness; Preparation; Preparing to be ready.

Remember at the beginning of this chapter when I told you about prepping my clients to have confidence? Confidence isn't the only thing a pageant girl needs. She also needs, well, of course, shoes!

As a pageant contestant begins to prepare for her onstage competitions, she needs to learn to walk in her high heels. The shoes must be prepared by practicing.

Wearing a new pair of shoes and breaking them in is essential to a pageant girl. If she doesn't practice in the shoes she will wear for competition a couple of terrible things could happen. She might not have broken in the shoes which will lead to her having horrible blisters on her feet. Or if she doesn't wear the right shoes to her gown fittings the hem of the gown may be too short. Finally, if she hasn't practiced perfecting her walk in the shoes she plans to wear during competition she will possibly lose her balance and may even fall.

Preparation.

Shoes of readiness.

Sports players need shoes prepared for the field, pageant girls need shoes prepared for the stage, soldiers need shoes prepared for battle, but warrior women of Christ need shoes prepared with readiness for the gospel of peace!

"Preach the word; be ready in season and out of season; rebuke, correct, and encourage with great patience and teaching."
2 Timothy 4:2 CSB

You see the part that says be ready in 2 Timothy 4:2?

In season and out of season, meaning at all times, we are to be ready. This battle armor piece is sandals of readiness but Ready for what?

Ready for the gospel of peace!

After I had battled my health issues for a while, I was filled with fear. Nothing in me was ready for anything. The only ready I felt was ready to see how it was all going to end. I knew I was done for. I was too far into the darkness of fear and settled into this "season" that had overtaken my world that I was incapable of readiness. I wasn't prepared for this battle. I had no armor. I had no clue where to get armor. If I'm completely honest, I had no desire to figure out how to go about preparing with this armor for battle, even if I could find it.

And that is where you, my friend, come into this part of my life. This is where even you, yes, the woman I may or may not know personally; even you have a place inside this story of God teaching me to prepare for battle!

I felt all alone during my fearful time. I don't know how to explain in words the depth of despair I was in. But I knew while I was suffering there was something great to come of this. And it's you! You are that great thing! I knew while I tried to fight there was someone who was going to need my story. It's you.

You are that special someone. I didn't know in the midst of my battle how crucial it was to be ready for the gospel of peace, but you will! I won't dare leave you on the battlefield facing the enemy without sharing first what God showed me in the midst of my battles.

You see each one of these chapters has been a struggle. A battle I knew I must face. I had no idea what would happen to get through these chapters but not far into writing this book God made it evident for me that I was going "walk it out before I wrote it out."

So here we go. Back to the gospel of peace.

Remember in chapter 4 when we read the Romans Road scriptures? Well, that's the story of the gospel of peace; the good news of Jesus.

You are now being challenged once more. Memorize this! Memorize as much and all of God's Word as possible!

We cannot prepare our feet with sandals of readiness for the gospel of peace if we don't know what the gospel of peace is!

Before Christ came, man had to obey God through laws that were given. Sacrifices were made to God, rituals were performed, and only the high priest was allowed to have direct communication with God Can you even imagine?! How difficult that would have been for me! I would've had to have slept right outside the temple gate and prepared to sacrifice daily for the atonement of my sins. Shew! I am so glad that is not what is required of us!

God also knew this was difficult for us! He knew we needed a way to be seen as clean before Him and that way was Jesus Christ.

We know from the Romans road scriptures that God sent His only son, born of a virgin, fully God, yet fully man, blameless and sinless walking the same earth our feet tread, and choosing to be the ultimate sacrifice for our sins so that because of His mercy and grace we could have access to the Father at anytime and anywhere and would have the gift of eternity in heaven!

All we have to do is confess with our mouth and believe in our hearts that Jesus is Lord and that this is the gospel of peace! Peace with God our creator!

And the enemy's strategy is to lie to you as you put on the belt of truth and the breastplate of righteousness. And right when you begin to lace up your sandals of readiness, oh, how he will try his best to stop you from knowing the gospel of truth.

He will begin to twist God's word, use it against you, slam your past in your face and lie to you saying every understanding and every Truth of God's Word you believe in is simply a myth.

Oh. But. You. Dear.

You will be ready! You will know and have God's word so stored in your heart that you will be able to correct the enemy and remind him who you are in Christ! You will be a Warrior Woman, standing against the enemy!

You see the enemy knows Christ. The demons know Christ. There is scripture after scripture where the demons saw Christ and feared Him; they begged Him not to torture them. They know the truth, but their father satan has them on a task to confuse you and use you, so you forget God's Word is the truth!

Jesus is the way, the truth, and the life!

As this chapter sat halfway written, I couldn't begin to finish it. I had no idea what to write next until something incredible happened. I received a nasty message on social media about my ministry group, Coffee and Jesus. I'll explain this group in another chapter. This message contained words saying Jesus wasn't who we think He is; he was merely a man who did kind things for others.

Oh boy! It took all I had not to respond and defend my Jesus right then and there! But I felt the Holy Spirit's tug to show love.

This time, unlike being lost in the battle of fear I faced before, I knew I had prepared my sandals of readiness. This time, I was ready and recognized the enemy's plot to try and get me to question my Jesus! I knew his tactics of wanting me to stop sharing the gospel of peace with anyone else!
Not this time, satan, not this time!

To know that God continues to be so faithful to me, that when I seek Him first when I prepare my battle armor to fight the attacks of the enemy the right way, Gods way, He is faithful to provide what I need. This reminds me all too well that this journey to becoming a strong, bold, and courageous warrior woman isn't about me at all. It's about God. It's about you and me preparing to do God's work!

Tighten your laces sister! We are halfway there!

Battle Plan #5
Designer Shoes

This battle plan is going to be slightly different than the others. It may even seem a little silly at first, but I want you to have a keepsake of sorts that you can look at every day before your day begins. I want this item to have such a profound meaning to you that when your eyes lock in on it, you are instantly reminded of who you are in Christ, what the truth of God's word is, and how you are about to begin the day marching into the battlefield, armed and ready!

Here is your battle plan:
You are going to create your very own pair of designer shoes. You can be as creative as you want to be with these, but there are a few rules.

Rule 1
At the end of Chapter 1 your first battle plan directed you to write down a scripture. This scripture must be included somewhere on your new shoes.

Rule 2
These shoes will not be worn, only placed somewhere you will see them before your day begins. So, fill them with memorable pieces of your battles, your past, your heart.

Rule 3
Remember when I shared with you how I trained my pageant clients to have confidence at the beginning of this chapter? Now, it is your turn. Go back and look at the rules and do this same thing. Find one promise of who you are in Christ, one talent God has given you to use to further His kingdom and write them both on your new shoes! You are the designer and the absolute BEST designer for your shoes! Make them

ready as you continue to memorize, study and equip yourself to become a Warrior Woman!

PS: Your shoes are YOURS. They should be as uniquely beautiful as you are! Be creative! Be brave! Be bold!

"And Abraham named that place The Lord Will Provide..."
Genesis 22:14

Chapter 6

Shield of Faith

Jehovah Jireh. These words have seemed apparent in my life lately and in the most unlikely ways have appeared numerous times.

In Genesis chapter 21 we read about the birth of Isaac, about how Hagar and Ishmael are sent away, and about the covenant made between Abraham and Abimelech.
Then in verse 1 of chapter 22, it says
"After these things" God tempted or tested Abraham.

The Hebrew word *Nissah* or *NahSah* translates to the English word tempt. Not meaning trying to make one do wrong; it means in the form of, to test or to prove the quality of.

What God is asking of Abraham in this text is to prove the quality of his obedience and faithfulness in God.

Pagans often sacrificed their children as offerings of food to their gods.
(See 2 Kings 16:3 and Ezekiel 23:37)

Having commanded Abraham to sacrifice Isaac was God seeking for him to demonstrate that Abraham was as willing to obey the true and only God as much as the pagans were committed to and willing to obey their gods.

God tells Abraham to take Isaac to the land of Moriah. We read this story and picture it as a quick happening as if it happened instantly. In our time everything happens fast, and we see this as a quick decision by Abraham to obey, God quickly intervenes, and then everyone lives happily ever after. The End.

Not the case.

You see, Abraham and Isaac were in a place called Beer Sheba. Beer Sheba means well of oath or well of seven; representing the covenant between Abraham and Abimelech. Abraham didn't just wake up the next morning and walk a few feet to the mountain. He had to travel for three days with Isaac. Three days! Can you even begin to fathom this occasion? Put yourself in place of Abraham for a moment. God has just asked you to sacrifice your child! A child He promised to you!

Let me pause here for a moment.

I want to share a bit of my testimony that until the past few weeks I have for the most part kept to myself. Lately, God has been working with me on not being selfish and sharing Jesus in every way I can. So here it is. When I was 17, I began having terrible female issues. I went to the doctor, and she placed me on birth control to help regulate hormones in hopes this would help. It didn't. I was diagnosed with a rare condition at the age of 18 that doctors said would prevent me from carrying a child full term, ever. Multiple people told me in the medical field that I would have numerous miscarriages and I would never carry a child past 34 weeks, resulting in premature delivery and potential health risks to a child. My husband and I found out we were four weeks pregnant only four weeks after we married. We were scared to say anything to anyone about the pregnancy for fear that we would lose our child. We decided to tell everyone because We knew we would have many praying. I prayed for God's will knowing His plan may not be our plan for this child, but we would accept that no matter the outcome.

This moment in our life was a real test of faith for us. Every appointment we had, took more prayers and courage of having faith that God would somehow perform a miracle. Every week that went by was another chance to praise Him. Every ultrasound was confirmation to us that God was providing a way for our child to grow.

I passed the first trimester, which is the point the doctors said if I could pass I should be able to carry my child until 30-34 weeks. We were thrilled! We questioned what would happen next but continued to have faith that God was in control.

At 34 weeks I chose to take a leave from my job and rest so my body could continue to nurture my growing healthy baby boy. My doctor wouldn't talk to me about what might happen at that point because she didn't know the answer, so I chose to change doctors. I kept faith in God knowing he would provide my body with everything it needed to carry my baby full term. I refused to believe my baby would be premature or have any health conditions preventing him from living the fullest life God intended.

We named our son, Kainen; our promise, the Warrior's son, a gift from God.

My doctors were astonished, my family was thankful, and my husband and I praised God for this blessing!

Today, we have a handsome, brilliant young man who loves Jesus wholeheartedly and seeks to love others as Christ does.

We recently celebrated his 14th Birthday!

To my knowledge, I am still the only patient at the hospital where I delivered my child to have a full term, healthy pregnancy, and deliver a child in perfect health, with my health condition.

My doctors contacted colleagues all across the country and never found anyone who had seen a case like this.

I tell you all these things because you need to know that God can and will provide the desires of your heart. I hope our story gives you strength to face the days ahead with full faithfulness in God. Praise Him! Believe Him! He knows His plans for you!

"Take delight in the Lord, and He will give you your heart's desires."
Psalm 37:4 HCSB

This reminds me so much of our lesson.
Let's see, where were we?
Oh yes, the traveling.
Abraham had to travel for three days.
You see Beer Sheba was about 50-60 miles from Moriah. This was not a short situation with a quick resolve. Oh, not at all. This travel must have been exhausting!

Abraham must have wondered what or how God would provide, but all the while still having faith that He would.

We can see Abraham's faithfulness immediately in the scripture because in verse three it says he rose up early in the morning.

Thinking of his obedience at this time encourages me. I am ever so quickly reminded of the times in my life where my battles have seemed so numerous, and yet I can look back now and see the lesson of faith, patience, and obedience being taught to me through them.

Think for a moment of your battles. Do you know of times God was strengthening you, testing your faith in Him?

Next is the most heartbreaking part of this story for me.

After three days of traveling, Abraham finally sees the mountain where God has told him to sacrifice Isaac. As they approach the mountain, his son, his promised blessing, looks to him to asks, "Where is the lamb?". The difficulty in this moment crushes me to the core. The anguish Abraham must have already been feeling, to then have his son recognize something is missing!

But his faithfulness and obedience continue.

The Bible mentions nothing of either of their feelings. Only the pureness of obedience of both Isaac and Abraham.

Abraham lifts the knife to sacrifice Isaac just as God has instructed and I'm confident with his heart pounding, yet remaining faithful that even if this goes all wrong, God will bring his promised son back to life

And right as he is about to finalize this act of obedience, God provides. Jehovah Jireh. An angel of the Lord calls out to him and stops him. Abraham opens his eyes and what else is before him but a ram, stuck in a thicket and ready to be sacrificed. Abraham calls the place of this mountain Jehovah Jireh, The Lord Will Provide!

Amazing isn't it? How our God, great and mighty, loves us so much that He provides our needs!

Our next battle piece is the shield of faith.

"In every situation take the shield of faith, and with it, you will be able to extinguish all the flaming arrows of the evil one."
Ephesians 6:16 HCSB

A Roman soldier's shield is not what you are probably imagining. My first thought would be a small, shiny arrow-shaped frame with a handle. Nope, think bigger. It's quite large. Sometimes up to 3 feet high and 3 feet wide!

That's much larger than I thought it would be!

It's called a scutum and has a large metal knob called a boss. It would have been rectangular shaped and slightly curved, making it a great form of protection for the soldier in battle; especially against any flaming darts!

Speaking of flaming darts and being guarded and protected, this takes me to another great story of faith, this time in the book of Daniel.

"He exclaimed, "Look! I see four men, not tied, walking around in the fire unharmed; and the fourth looks like a son of the gods."
Daniel 3:25 HCSB

It took boldness and courage for these three to walk in faith. Shadrach, Meshach, and Abednego denied bowing to any other god, but the Holy, Almighty, Lord of All! Yahweh, The Great I Am!

They knew that no matter what they faced, whether fire or death or miraculous salvation, their God was with them; they would praise Him only.

Then after the furnace was heated seven times greater than usual, as things began to get hot, so hot that the men throwing them in were burned up, these three were tossed inside to die!

But what happens next is where you and I can have hope!

The Bible says that King Nebuchadnezzar looks into the furnace and sees not only the three but one more. A fourth person. Jesus.

Jesus was with them in the midst of the fire. While the one seated on the earthly throne was watching and waiting upon their destruction, there was Jesus, protecting them from the flames.

They were so significantly protected that not only did these men escape burns, but nothing of them even smelled like fire!

What is our shield of faith? It's the faith we have in Jesus Christ. Knowing that like Abraham was promised Isaac, we were promised Christ. And just as Abraham knew God would provide a sacrifice, we have hope in the ultimate sacrifice, Jesus Christ!

A friend recently shared with me Hebrews 11.

It is subtitled heroes of faith in my bible. What a proper heading. The book of Hebrews is filled with reminders of people like Abraham, Moses, and Enoch. People of great faith! Look at verse 1 with me!

"Now faith is the reality of what is hoped for, the proof of what is not seen."
Hebrews 11:1 HCSB

Abraham didn't see the ram until it was time.
Shadrach, Meshach, and Abednego didn't see a way out of the fire.
Moses didn't see a way to the other side of the Red Sea.
But in all these stories faith is what was shown.
And God provided!

Jehovah Jireh!

We may not see Jesus in the flesh as the disciples did, but we can have faith knowing that one day the sky will open, and we will be called to our Heavenly Father for eternity with Him! That shield of faith, the very one the enemy will try to destroy, is the first piece of armor you won't wear, but yet, you must pick it up yourself and carry it!

Are you ready?
Do you know Jesus Christ?
Do you have faith in Him so intense that your arms can carry the weight of this shield and you can use it to stop the enemy's fiery darts?

Pick up your shield and let's keep preparing for battle!

Battle Plan #6
Your extinguisher

You learned in this chapter that the enemy will be shooting his fiery darts at you, therefore, we know we have to be prepared for them. You have to be ready and watching for them. It isn't a matter of when they will be shot, but understanding that they will come, they will be hot, and you will need to fully aware and prepped!

1.   Think of a moment your faith was tested. How did you handle this situation? Did you rely on your faith? Do you feel you passed the test?

2.   I want you to find scriptures about your faith. Study them and memorize them. You choose the one that God speaks to you in and put it on a note in the front of your bible.

3.   Lastly, for this battle plan, you need to share your own testimony. It doesn't have to be everything about your life and walk with Christ, but this week pay attention to those who you cross paths with and encourage them to grow in faith by sharing a relative and personal testimony.

"But He said to them, "Why are you fearful, you of little faith?" Then He got up and rebuked the winds and the sea. And there was a great calm."

Matthew 8:26

Chapter 7

Helmet of Salvation

For two years I have faced a battle that has taken me down roads of loneliness, roads of defeat, roads of heartbreak, roads of pain and roads of desperation.

Never did I ever imagine or even begin to fathom pondering what it would be like to have someone give me a small bit of hope in a medical answer, but today that is what I found.

As you've followed along preparing your armor you've read my story of preparing mine. Not a former story, not a past situation, but a current one. You've been walking this path step by step with me. As God has unfolded each move, each unwinding of the next place on my personal battle field, I have simultaneously written.

Remember, I told you I had to walk it out before I could write it out.

Sunshine came through today! Less than a week ago my chiropractor sent me to have some testing and today I received the results of that test. I won't reveal the results just yet because they are merely numbers without explanation for now. But I have a next step, I have finally seen some movement in this long health process.

These results, although sending me on another journey with another doctor, these results are happiness. Happiness to me because something IS wrong with me. I giggle out loud as I write that sentence. Yes, I am praising Jesus today because my blood work finally shows something abnormal after days, months, and years of doctors looking at me like I am crazy!

I read a quote today that said, "Honor the space between 'no longer' and 'not yet'"!

That's exactly where I see myself. In that unknown place again but ever so thankful for the place between no longer wondering what is going on with me and the place of not yet holding the exact answer. Today was a moment of victory in this battle!

Although the battle isn't over, I can cling to the promises of Christ in this and see even the smallest victories! Today was a taste of deliverance!

As we move into the next part of preparing our armor we will see this is the final piece we are to wear. The helmet of salvation. The protection of our deliverance.

But first this reminds me of a night the disciples' faith was shaken and how the enemy wants to shake our faith as well.

"As He got into the boat, His disciples followed Him. Suddenly, a violent storm arose on the sea, so that the boat was being swamped by the waves. But He was sleeping. So the disciples came and woke Him up, saying, "Lord, save us! We're going to die!" But He said to them, "Why are you fearful, you of little faith?" Then He got up and rebuked the winds and the sea. And there was a great calm. The men were amazed and asked, "What kind of man is this? — even the winds and the sea obey Him!"
Matthew 8:23-27 HCSB

The last few weeks the word anxiety has come up in many conversations. I've talked with friends who are anxious, I've talked with family members who are anxious, I've even been anxious myself!

I noticed a common thread in every conversation about anxiety; the fear was coming from a place of doubt.

It got me thinking about the night described in the book of Matthew.

Let me set the scene for you, the disciples have just witnessed miracle after miracle. A man was healed from a skin disease, a servant healed from paralysis, and even Peter's mother in law was healed from fever!

After all of those miracles occurred many who were demon possessed were brought to Jesus and healed.

After seeing these miracles surely, the disciples would have strong faith in Jesus!

Right?

Wrong.

The next events that unfold are eerily scary!

Jesus gets on a boat with the disciples and crosses to the other side of the sea.

Picture this for a moment: it's dark, it's storming, and they are surrounded by water!

That's enough terror for one night, in my opinion! But there is more to it than even this mild description.

This storm wasn't a gentle breeze and a little rain either! It's described as a raging storm! A fierce windstorm that was tossing waves that were breaking over the boat! The disciples were scared!!

S. C. A. R. E. D.

Scared!

Anxiety! Fear! Terror!

All the while Jesus is sleeping!

Why isn't He worried while this storm rages against the boat?

"Doesn't He care?" (The disciples asked Him.)

He isn't worried because He knows He holds the authority over the storm!

Jesus got up and said, "Be still!", and guess what happened? The wind obeyed Him! The sea quieted!

Aren't we the same as the disciples when we focus on the wind and the storms of our lives instead of on the one we know holds the authority over everything?

We become so full of anxiety that we forget all the miracles we've witnessed our Savior perform!

That, my warrior sister, is what you call enemy strategy; to make us forget the truth of Jesus!

He knows we are sealed by the Holy Spirit, so the enemy uses every fiery dart he can to make us forget the power in Jesus!

Scripture tells us the enemy comes to kill, steal and destroy but that Jesus came to give life abundantly!! (John 10:10)

Just like the faith of the disciples are shaken in this moment, the enemy wants us to be shaken in our faith in Jesus as well.

This is where our helmet of salvation comes in.

We must know to whom we belong!

Let's study the Roman soldier's helmet and see its physical comparison to our spiritual helmet of salvation.

I believe it's safe to say that we know there was no such thing as mass production or factory lines during the time of the Roman soldiers. Therefore, we know that no two helmets were exactly identical either.

However, these helmets were all made to be strong and with the same intended purpose; protect the head from the enemy's attack.

Imagine walking into an art museum and seeing a beautifully crafted metal piece that grabs your attention with its intricate carvings, its spectacular engravings, and its elaborate design. A piece so inspiring you become engulfed in its beauty! That same intrigue would probably capture us if we watched Roman soldiers walking by with their helmets.

How perfect that the same beautiful, intricately crafted, elaborate and inspiring physical helmet that Paul compares in this scripture is given to us through our spiritual helmet of salvation! And when we are confident in wearing it and it is tightly wrapped around our head snuggly fit in place, you will become one well noticed warrior woman! People will want to know where you obtained this, how you got it, and what they need to do to get it!

Speaking of a snug fit, let's study this word a little deeper.

Helmet.

The Greek word for helmet, *Perikephalaia,* is composed from two root words, *peri* and *kephale. Peri* meaning around and *kephale* meaning head. So, the Greek word for helmet literally means 'around the head'.

I dare say this proves to us how important this helmet is in both the physical and spiritual forms.

During a battle the soldier's helmet surrounds his entire head for protection. Sometimes these helmets went as far as having cheek plates, a brow ridge and a metal plate down the neck to protect to back of the head and neck. Every part of the head was surrounded by protection.

The same applies in the spiritual helmet
of salvation. We must know, without doubt, God's promises for us who are living abundantly in Christ.

The Roman soldier's helmet protects the brain.
A warrior woman's helmet protects the mind.

The question isn't how the enemy will make his next attack on you, but when! Be prepared, Warrior Sister!

Your mind is your battlefield, the enemy is looking for every way he can to destroy you by planting seeds of doubt in you.

Be alert and aware of these!

Remember reading 1 Peter 5:8?

If you don't then you should and that is your next challenge. Start memorizing scripture that reminds you of exactly who you are in Christ!

We will NOT be weak women!

We will be warrior women, who know the promises of their Commander!

Tighten your helmet, friend! Make sure it is securely in place!

Snug like a bug in a rug!

We are about to finish this with a sword fight!

Battle Plan #7
Finding Promises

As we come closer to the end of preparing our armor for battle, you will possibly begin to experience even stronger attacks from the enemy. No need to worry, Jesus has this under control. How do I know? Because in training to secure my helmet, I had to go on a treasure hunt for God's promises.

Now, its your turn!

1.   During your study time this week, search for times where life seemed out of control until Jesus arrived. I've already mentioned a few throughout this book, but don't use those. Find others so you can challenge yourself to "dig" for that perfect treasure piece. Write the scriptures in your warrior notebook and reference them any time you feel your helmet may need a little securing.

2.   Once you've discovered your perfect jewel moment, next, search for scriptures that remind you of who you are in Christ. Write them in your warrior notebook.

3.   Finally, your treasure box (your mind) needs to be filled to the top. This time your search is to find scriptures that prove there is nothing you can do to earn your salvation and there is nothing the enemy can do to take it away. Again, write them in your notebook and come back to them when your helmet seems a little loose.

This is the full image of Sylvia's painting displayed in her office at New Life Assembly of God in Woodstock, Alabama. It is comprised of several individual canvas paintings that create her beautiful artwork.

"In the beginning was the Word, and the Word was with God, and the Word was God."

John 1:1

Chapter 8
The Sword of the Spirit

Our journey together thus far has been all about what we wear; the armor that we put on. We are about to embark into new territory during this next preparation step as we go from securing our battle attire to being armed and ready with our most fierce weapon of all: The Sword!

Paul has taught so far in Ephesians 6 what we are to put on, but in verse 17 he says, "take the helmet of salvation and the sword of the spirit." So here we go, girlfriend! We have been repositioned from recruit to soldier! How exciting is this going to be?!

Before we go into the battlefield with our sword we must be trained on how to properly handle a weapon of this magnitude. You see, what you have just been given is THE weapon of ALL weapons. No longer are we only covered in gear to protect ourselves from the enemy's attacks, but we are now presented with defense!

Let's look at one of my favorite warriors and train accordingly.

Our warrior is David. We all know the story for the most part I would imagine. However, since there might be some very new soldiers amongst us and since those of us who may be wearing slightly weathered armor could use a little refreshing, let's take a look at the background of this warrior David.

In 1 Samuel chapter 16, Saul is the reigning king, but because of his disobedience, God has summoned Samuel to anoint a new king.

Move forward a bit and Samuel is with Jesse and his sons. Jesse calls them each forward one by one. Men of great stature appear before Samuel, but as each one is presented before him, Samuel knows they are not the one God wants anointed as king.

Jesse presents them all to Samuel, but one. David. Humble, young shepherd boy, David.

Now, there's no way he would ever be chosen, right? He's the youngest, most likely the smallest, possibly even less mature than the others. God can choose anyone to be appointed as king, so surely He isn't going to anoint David. After all, David is by the world's standards not, well to put it kindly, "king material".

But 1 Samuel 16:7 tells us a different story!

By the way this is my favorite verse of the Bible!

"But the Lord said to Samuel, "Do not look at his appearance or his stature, because I have rejected him. Man does not see what the Lord sees for man sees what is visible, but the Lord sees the heart.""
1 Samuel 16:7 HCSB

This scripture is referring to one of David's brothers, Eliab, but it gives us great insight as to the qualities God is searching for in His next king and looks are not at the top of the list.

God knew David's heart. He knew that David was humble, meek, teachable, willing, a servant, and yes, a warrior!!!

How could David NOT be chosen as king?!

After he is anointed some of his brothers are sent to war against the Philistines, while David continues to tend to sheep. Until one day when his father sends him to take food to his brothers.

When David arrives, the army is in battle formation shouting their battle cry! He runs to his brothers and asks how they are, then, in the same moment, Goliath shows up!

Here David is faced with his giant for the very first time. This nine-foot nine-inch giant of a man in all his mockery now stands before young David, the shepherd boy. Scripture tells us that all the men retreated because they were terrified! But David is about to show what happens to those protected by God.

David had spoken to one of the Israelite men who tells him about how the king is going to reward the one who defeats this giant. The victor will be given a wife and riches and he will never pay taxes again! Friend, I don't know about you but not having to pay taxes alone sounds like enough to grab my attention!

I love David's next words! In verse 26 he asks one of the most powerful questions in his entire story!

"Just who is the uncircumcised Philistine that he should defy the armies of the living God?"

Whew-wee! Talk about defending the honor of the Lord! David was ready, so ready that he ran to the giant!

Ran to the giant!

Pause here for a moment with me and let's ponder this situation! I want you to truly grasp what is happening here! David is RUNNING to his giant!

Who are you in your battles?

Do you become like the Israelite army and retreat in fear and terror? Or do you face this thing head on like David did, running toward the giant ready to wage war against him?

Here's the part we must be aware of; David knew what God's promise was to his people! He knew God had given the Israelites the promised land that this giant was blocking and because of that knowledge, because of remembering who he was and what belonged to him, because of that, David could face this Philistine giant without trembling!

Before David reaches victory though he does face adversity. First, David's very own brother accuses him of arrogance and having an evil heart! Wow! I'm sure each of us have been there, too! Now, you and I know this whole story of David already and so we know that God has chosen David to be elevated to a position of leadership and authority based upon his heart, not upon anything else! And that is all the proof we need to confirm this is yet a tactic of the enemy trying to wreck Gods plan!

Isn't that usually how things work for us as well?! Right when we are feeling suited up and ready for battle the enemy swoops in with his conniving, deceitful schemes trying to mess us all up and confuse us from standing firm on God's word and His promises to us!

Then, if that isn't enough he sends in the very person David will take the throne from to make him feel inadequate! Saul tells David there is no way he is going to defeat this giant! And then he tells David every reason why he can't!

"You're too young! This Philistine has been a warrior all his life!"

Adversity before a battle has the potential to leave you feeling defeated before the fight ever begins!

But David doesn't hear any of it! Not a word! He quickly reminds Saul that he has essentially prepared for this moment all his life too! He's been in the field protecting sheep; striking down and killing their enemies like bears and lions! David also did not forgetthe most important part of his training; it is God who has him covered! In verse 37 David says *"The Lord who rescued me from the the paw of the lion and the paw of the bear will rescue me from the hand of this Philistine!"*

And God does! David runs to the battlefield armed and ready! He takes out a stone and knocks Goliath to the ground!

What does all of this have to do with us being equipped with the sword of the spirit?

David runs over to the giant on the ground, takes the giants sword out of the sheath and uses this very weapon formed to harm David to kill this Philistine giant once and for all!

Did you catch that?

THE weapon the giant thought he was going to use against David, ended up being exactly the weapon God equips David with to finish this fight!

Honey, you better write this down until it is buried in your mind so deep nothing can take it from you:

"No weapon formed against you will succeed, and you will refute any accusation raised against you in court. This is the heritage of the Lord's servants, and their righteousness is from Me." This is the Lord's declaration."
Isaiah 54:17 HCSB

Just as God provided a sword for David's battle, He has also equipped us with one!

You may be going through a battle that seems endless right now, but believe me, sister, with God on your side the enemy will lose, and you will have victory!

Look back for a minute to verse 16.

"Every morning and evening for 40 days the philistine came forward and took his stand."

40 days of mockery ends with a sword fight!

Hmmm, reminds me of another time the enemy tries to use God's word to make a mockery of Him!

Matthew chapter 4 tells the story of Jesus in the wilderness. The purpose of this temptation from satan is to prove to us that Jesus was human, to give us an example of how to handle temptation, and to give Jesus the opportunity to confirm God's plan.

But what we must key in on here is how satan tries to tempt Jesus.

Jesus had been in the wilderness for 40 days and 40 nights when satan tempts him for the first time. Jesus had also been fasting and scripture confirms to us that he was hungry! What better way for satan to begin this mockery and temptation than to start with the very thing Jesus' human body needed and desired, food.

"Then the tempter approached Him and said, "If You are the Son of God, tell these stones to become bread.""
Matthew 4:3 HCSB
And do you want to know how Jesus fought this?
Yep, with the sword of the spirit!

"But He answered, "It is written: Man must not live on bread alone but on every word that comes from the mouth of God.""
Matthew 4:4 HCSB

That simple move is actually one of great authority and power! Jesus needed only to use God's word to remind satan of who He was!
Jesus is tempted a second time and this time satan tries to use the same weapon against Jesus that Jesus had just used against him.
He takes Jesus to the holy city, places him on the pinnacle of the temple and quotes scripture to Jesus to get him to prove who he is.
"and said to Him, "If You are the Son of God, throw Yourself down. For it is written: He will give His angels orders concerning you, and they will support you with their hands so that you will not strike your foot against a stone.""
Matthew 4:6 HCSB

Now, make a note here. The enemy knows our weapon and he will try to use it against us, which makes it ever so important for us to study, memorize, train, and know how to use this weapon properly!

If satan knows the scriptures, shouldn't we?

Jesus knows His own authoritative position and He doesn't need the enemy tempting Him with what He knows He can already do!
Jesus responds:

"Jesus told him, "It is also written: Do not test the Lord your God.""
Matthew 4:7 HCSB

Finally, in a last attempt, satan places Jesus on a mountain and offers Him all He can see, but Jesus knows who He is and tells satan to back off!

"Then Jesus told him, "Go away, Satan! For it is written: Worship the Lord your God, and serve only Him.""
Matthew 4:10

Do you see why it is severely important that we train, understand, and practice using the sword of the spirit before our battles?

Jesus knew exactly what God's word said and so should we! When you bury your face in God's word and begin to store it in your heart and apply it to your life, then you will be prepared for battles against our enemy!

David fought with a physical sword that God equipped him with, but like we are to do, Jesus fought with a spiritual sword that God has equipped us with in battle!

A Roman soldier's sword called a *gladius*, was made of steel and used in war. It was both a defensive and offensive weapon. It could be used to protect from attack and to attack and kill the enemy.

The same applies to our Sword! It can protect us from the enemy's attack and it can be used to fight the enemy in war!

Look at these next few scriptures throughout the Bible that speaks of God's word:

"All Scripture is inspired by God and is profitable for teaching, for rebuking, for correcting, for training in righteousness, so that the man of God may be complete, equipped for every good work."

2 Timothy 3:16-17 HCSB

"I have treasured Your word in my heart so that I may not sin against You."
Psalms 119:11 HCSB

"Your word is a lamp for my feet and a light on my path."
Psalms 119:105 HCSB

"For the word of God is living and effective and sharper than any double-edged sword, penetrating as far as the separation of soul and spirit, joints and marrow. It is able to judge the ideas and thoughts of the heart."
Hebrews 4:12 HCSB

Sister, you have now been given knowledge of the most powerful piece of your battle armor. Pick up your sword! Learn it! Know it! Keep it hidden in your heart! Be ready to use it! Train yourself, Warrior Every. Single. Day. Train!

A brief update:
I want to share some change in my personal battle before moving into the next chapter with you.
Last I wrote you about my health I had found a bit of hope and would be sent to a specialist.
What we have discovered is I have an autoimmune disease called Hashimoto's Thyroiditis. I've been given medication to help treat this and a little more hope that I should soon begin feeling somewhat back to my normal self. I share this story with you because I want you to be part of my joys as you have also been reading my weakness in this fight. I want to encourage you to tell your own story. It doesn't have to be in a book, you don't even have to write it out, but please at least speak it. A friend shared a saying with me a few days ago that has stuck in my mind; "Share your story, even if your voice is shaking"

What powerful words! Many times in our lives the enemy can attack us in a way he shuts us up, but don't let him win that fight! God has given you your exact story for a purpose. Someone else needs to know there is someone struggling just like them! Be someone else's hope. Let Jesus shine through your story.

Imagine the stories the enemy has played a part in keeping secret. We are to be light in a dark world. It reminds me of the scripture in the book of Matthew where Jesus teaches us to be light.

""You are the light of the world. A city situated on a hill cannot be hidden. No one lights a lamp and puts it under a basket, but rather on a lampstand, and it gives light for all who are in the house. In the same way, let your light shine before men, so that they may see your good works and give glory to your Father in heaven."
Matthew 5:14-16 HCSB

Since you have been called into the family and kingdom of the Most-High God, The Almighty, The Great I Am, you are now light, a story of hope, and a representative of Jesus Christ! Share your story sister and prepare your sword!

Our armor is in place, but we are not yet ready! Over the next two chapters you and I are going to learn to fight using two more strategies that cannot be overlooked.

Secure your armor and let's start more training!

Battle Plan #8
Battle Cry

This battle plan will seem simple at first, it may even begin to become repetitive and boring at times, but it must be taken extremely seriously!

You are now going to write every scripture that has been mentioned in this book.

Not here. You will need a brand-new notebook with empty pages. You are going to memorize them all through the process of writing them daily!

Get your notebook and pen ready and write them down word for word. As you write them, speak them loudly! What we speak is heard by the heavens and by the enemies of God!

This is your Battle Cry!

Battle Cry: a word or phrase shouted by soldiers going into battle to express solidarity and intimidate the enemy.

I love that last part.... Intimidate the enemy!

"He Himself bore our sins in His body on the tree, so that, having died to sins, we might live for righteousness; you have been healed by His wounds."

1 Peter 2:24 HCSB

Chapter 9

Prayer

I'm writing this from the emergency room bed while I am waiting to be admitted to room 404. It's cold and I am a bit concerned about what the next few hours may hold. I know I just shared with you that I had finally found hope, and I did, then strange things began to happen.

For months, years actually, I've imagined a day like this taking place. Today started as any other day would, I woke up to do my Coffee and Jesus devotion, only to find myself drained even after a great night of sleep.

Oh, and I promise this will be the chapter that I share with you the story of the Coffee and Jesus group.

Instead of getting up I laid back in the bed listening to one of my many devotion apps until at some point in time I fell asleep; most likely between the end of the Old Testament Scripture reading and the actual devotion.

I woke back up feeling fine. I took my thyroid medicine with water, called my mom to see if she had coffee and woke up my son to get our day started.

Moments later I'd find myself in the same place I'd been many times before during this battle, and 3 times within the past 4 days with these specific symptoms: weakness on my right side, numbness in my face, and the weirdest feeling of pressure in my ear.

Pause here: my transport friend just came in to move me to my new room for the night.

What a night! I know as you read this it may be a little hard to follow, but I am now writing to you from our grandparents' river home. I know,

I know, it's a bit unusual, but time has allowed me to collect my thoughts and all information to finish this story for you.

Where were we?

Oh yes, they moved me to my hospital room.

I was finally given a room for the night, but this stay was far from a 5 Star hotel with comfy pillows and a fluffy bedspread. I was poked on, woken up for blood work, and tested for everything under the sun! I'm not complaining though. I'm thankful for a very quick reacting hospital staff.

When I arrived that afternoon to the emergency room I was having stroke symptoms, and in my family, you don't take that lightly. My family history includes my maternal grandmother having multiple TIAs or mini strokes, and my mother having a stroke in 2008 due to high blood pressure. We don't play around with stroke symptoms and I am thankful the hospital staff doesn't either.

Every test that night showed nothing unusual. No tumors, no aneurysms, no stroke, no signs of blockage, the repetitive answer of the night was no! And that was great news, but to get to these no answers I had to face a fear I have had for two years:

The MRI Tunnel

Now, I'm not typically claustrophobic, but the thought of being trapped in that machine has truly terrified me for more than two years.

This time I knew I had no other choice but to face this fear!

I waited for more than 3 hours after the doctor ordered my testing before I was actually wheeled to the dungeon.

Insert dungeon music here.

I'm only kidding. I was taken to a room with a very precious nurse taking care of me. Jeremy was able to follow us there, but he had to stay in the waiting area until the tests were over.

As I was moved from one bed to another to be placed inside this tunnel the nurse explained I would be in there for 2 hours!

What? TWO HOURS!!

I have had this fear built inside me for what seemed to be an eternity, because I didn't want to be in that thing for 20 minutes, and I am being told right before I go in that I have to face two hours of this terror! I knew there was only one thing that would get me through this test.

PRAYER!

Girlfriend, I began to pray and praise the Lord like never before! With all the banging and clanging of this horrific machine in my ears, I was drawn into a place a worshiping our Heavenly Father that left me with no words to completely explain the depth of what happened between Jesus and I in the dreaded place I feared for so long.

I couldn't move so I was stuck completely in my mind singing to my Jesus! I sang song after song to Him and then I prayed and praised Him more than ever before! Tears pour down my face as I share these details of one of the most intimate moments I have ever experienced with our Savior! I prayed for my husband, our son, my parents, his parents, our family, friends, the ladies in Coffee and Jesus, any and every one that came to mind, including you! Yes, in what seemed to be the darkest moment at that time, I planted my face on the ground at the foot of the throne of our precious Savior and I prayed for Him to rise up a nation of Warrior Women!! Sister, when I left that tunnel of darkness I felt the overflowing power of Jesus Christ! There was no way I was accepting defeat in this battle! I knew something wasn't correct in my body, but I believed with all my heart that in that moment, whatever it was would be fixable and I would be healed.

I find absolutely no coincidence in the fact that as I write this to you in the note section of my cell phone, a notification from my bible app appears across my screen with the scripture of the day:

"He Himself bore our sins in His body on the tree, so that, having died to sins, we might live for righteousness; you have been healed by His wounds."
1 Peter 2:24 HCSB

My Sweet Jesus! How gracious and loving you are to us!

My tests came back with NO!

Every. Single. Time.

No, to multiple sclerosis.
No, to stroke.
No, to an aneurysm.
No, to tumors.
No, to vascular blockage.
No, to heart disease.
No, No, and No!

My Jesus!

That is why I heard the word NO over and over!

In those two hours what could have been spent in fear I spent in prayer. And that's the very first of our last two strategies we will train and equip ourselves with before we go into the battle and conquer.

In Ephesians 6 Paul's final words of putting on armor end this way;
"Pray at all times in the Spirit with every prayer and request, and stay alert in this with all perseverance and intercession for all the saints. Pray also for me, that the message may be given to me when I open my mouth to make known with boldness the mystery of the gospel. For this I am an ambassador in chains. Pray that I might be bold enough in Him to speak as I should."

Ephesians 6:18-20 HCSB

Again, we see the word *Pray* repeated three times, just as we read the word *Stand* three times in the earlier portion of the Ephesian 6 scriptures.

The number three signifies a few meanings; it is a number reflecting completion or perfection and is thought to be a number symbolizing growth.

The number three is also significant in our next lesson of prayer.

Jesus prayed in the garden of Gethsemane three times. (*Matthew 26:44*)

The word Gethsemane is made up of two Hebrew words; GAT and SHMANIM. Gethsemane means "the place where olive oil is pressed".

In order for olives to be pressed into oil, they must endure a great amount of pressure. The more pressure created, the more oil received. Throughout the Bible, oil symbolizes the presence of the Spirit of God. Stay with me on this topic, we are going to go a little deeper into our study with these two Hebrew words.

The Hebrew word GAT alone means a winepress. SHMANIN, meaning oils, is the plural form of the Hebrew word SHEMEN, meaning oil. Combined, these two words literally mean, winepress of oils. Wine is symbolic of joyfulness and gladness.

Many times, in scripture oil and wine are used together to represent God's favor. In the book of Joel, chapter 2, the Lord is seeking repentance from His people in Judah and He promises new oil and wine for His people.

Joel has shouted God's warning in chapter one and partly in chapter 2. During this time of locust devouring the land, three losses are mentioned, due to the locust attack; wine, grain, and oil.

In Joel 1:5, the loss of wine is spoken of because the locust destroyed the grapevines. Then in verse nine, grain and drink offerings are cut off from the house of the Lord, and finally in verses ten, eleven, and twelve oil fails and all access to food and drink are devoured and withered away.

Physically the people have lost what they desire, their food for survival, and their access to the presence of God.

We can view this in a spiritual manner, grain being God's word, wine being the joyfulness of the Lord, and the oil representing the presence of God.

For the Israelites, grain and drink offerings brought before the Lord allowed them access to God's presence. For us, Jesus became the ultimate sacrifice so that we could forever be in the Lord's presence.

Our communication line with our Father, our prayers, are only available because of Jesus and the very battle He prayed about three times in the Garden of Gethsemane.

"Then Jesus came with them to a place called Gethsemane, and He told the disciples, "Sit here while I go over there and pray." Taking along Peter and the two sons of Zebedee, He began to be sorrowful and deeply distressed. Then He said to them, "My soul is swallowed up in sorrow—to the point of death. Remain here and stay awake with Me." Going a little farther, He fell facedown and prayed, "My Father! If it is possible, let this cup pass from Me. Yet not as I will, but as You will." Then He came to the disciples and found them sleeping. He asked Peter, "So, couldn't you stay awake with Me one hour? Stay awake and pray, so that you won't enter into temptation. The spirit is willing, but the flesh is weak. Again, a second time, He went away and prayed, "My Father, if this cannot pass unless I drink it, Your will be done." And He came again and found them sleeping because they could not keep their eyes open. After leaving them, He went away again and prayed a third time, saying the same thing once

more. Then He came to the disciples and said to them, "Are you still sleeping and resting? Look, the time is near. The Son of Man is being betrayed into the hands of sinners. Get up; let's go! See, My betrayer is near."

Matthew 26:36-46
During this night Jesus prays the same prayer three times. He asks God to remove the burden of the battle from Him if at all possible, but each time He continues to pray God's will be done, not His own. Like the meaning of Gethsemane, Jesus was placed under pressure in order that you and I might never be separated from God. He took on our sins to save us from suffering and separation.

Paul tells us to stay alert in prayer. During the night Jesus was praying the disciples fell asleep, over and over and over. We must be alert at all times and in prayer at all times, spiritually equipped for battle against the enemy. Our strength comes from the Lord and our relationship, our prayers and communication with Him, determine our readiness for the fight to defeat the enemy through Christ!
Paul's message ends with possibly THE most important message; to pray!

Prayer is our communication with God! It's the way we build a relationship with Him!

Our Savior, Jesus Christ, has already been victorious over the enemy. If we know we have victory in Christ and that His voice leads His sheep (John 10:27), then this also confirms to us that we must have a means of connection in order to know how to follow. Prayer is your direct line to the commander. You can't attack the enemy without the voice of a commander telling you when and how!

Prayer connects you to God and ultimately, because of Christ, gives YOU power over the enemy.

Coffee and Jesus

I promised to share the story about the Coffee and Jesus devotion group with you before this chapter was over, so here it is.

I wrote early in the book about a change that happened in me during Spring 2017. I knew the Lord was calling me to lead women to Jesus. I knew what He asked and for weeks (probably months) I fought Him.

After experiencing the most sickening feeling in my stomach for days for not obeying, I caved. I did what God asked me to do and that was to start a women's ministry on facebook to write devotions and share my passion of studying God's word! Coffee and Jesus devotion group was birthed! Since September 4, 2017, I have shared the devotions and studies God has placed on my heart with women across the globe.

There are days I struggle with waking up extra early to study and to be honest I want to stay in my warm bed and sleep. There are days want to quit because I feel inadequate to be sharing God's word. There are days I want to delete my entire account because my personal struggles consume me, and I can't bear facing these ladies with tears in my eyes. But I know that God has called me to do a task He is qualifying me for.

I can't do this. But He alone can.

There's nothing special that I've done in my life to have the skills or qualifications that I need to lead this. But God does!

I am not someone who most would consider knowledgeable in God's word. But God most certainly is, after all, it's His Word! What started from an act of obedience has turned into something that can only point to Jesus Christ. I thought when this all started there would be maybe 20, give or take, of my closest family and friends joining me each weekday to hear God's message. Little did I know, God had other plans, plans much bigger than I ever imagined.

Today, there are more than 4100 women in Coffee and Jesus, every single state is represented and there are now 33 countries represented too!

WHOA! This is insane! This is God in action! There's nothing I could possibly do to create this! I'm merely a little country gal from Woodstock, Alabama! But My God is powerful! He is wonderful! He is plentiful! He provides! He knows all! He is faithful! God is so, so good! If He is telling you to make a move, then Do It! Now! Don't worry with what everyone else thinks or what they will say! Allow God to move before you in His calling and trust that He WILL provide for you, and YOU be certain everything you do points people to Jesus! Thank you, Father, for being so gracious to me! The enemy has tried to stop me many times during these past few months, but I am strong and ONLY BECAUSE OF JESUS CHRIST! Jesus Christ is my everything!

"so My word that comes from My mouth will not return to Me empty, but it will accomplish what I please and will prosper in what I send it to do.""
Isaiah 55:11 HCSB

"Go, therefore, and make disciples of all nations, baptizing them in the name of the Father and of the Son and of the Holy Spirit,"
Matthew 28:19 HCSB

"For nothing will be impossible with God.""
Luke 1:37 HCSB

Sister, follow Jesus! He is ALL you need!

Battle Plan #9
Power in Prayer

This battle plan will be created by you diligently searching scriptures on prayer.

I can't walk this for you, nor can you walk my prayer road for me. This is the time you must focus on being alone with God and building your relationship with Him.

I will be praying for you always.

Find a quiet space in your home and create a prayer time each day.

Begin praying all during the day as well.

Pray about everything. You will find yourself strong and ready for battle after spending time with God alone.

Look at what happened to Moses when He was in the presence of the Lord. He was glowing!

Sister, the enemy will know He can't stand against you, when you spend time with The Great I Am!

So we do not focus on what is seen, but on what is unseen. For what is seen is temporary, but what is unseen is eternal."

2 Corinthians 4:18 HCSB

Chapter 10

Fasting

We made it! We are about to complete our final stage of preparing for battle! Before we move into the topic at hand, I want to share something I wrote to the ladies of Coffee and Jesus. I believe in being as transparent as possible in order to fully encourage and strengthen one another. We live in a world that seems to think we should display perfection and that any form of the lack thereof is a sign of weakness. However, I know differently. During my times of fasting God has allowed me to see how I need to share all of me with others, because perfection is a lie, and in order for me to become a leader of women for Christ, the fullness of struggles must be shown.

"Good morning! I want to be as honest and real with y'all as possible. I'm fighting a battle right now that is hard to deal with, but I am working through this with prayer and fasting and trying to have patience to know God is fighting for me. I know the truth in this battle will be revealed in His timing and I know He sees all, hears all, and knows all. But while I'm in the midst of this fight I would appreciate your prayers. Following Jesus isn't always easy. Doing what God has called you to do isn't always a "walk in the park". Today, I am struggling, and simply ask that you pray for me to remain in the strength of Jesus. I'm not here to pretend or be perfect. I'm here to share life you, real, hardcore, heart opened, spiritual battling, Christ following life. Please forgive me for delaying our devotion today. I know I am an overcomer in Christ, it's just taking a little longer today than usual to let that sink in. I love y'all and I thank you for covering me in prayer!"

I don't remember exactly what was happening that particular day but I do remember as I fasted at the beginning of the year I was pelted with one attack after another. It was hard! I want you to prepare for these moments. You are going to have victory, but you are also going to find yourself in days of valley defeat! Trying moments, you won't expect, that will happen when you think you are fully ready for anything. This is why we must focus on what the Lord is asking of us and we must not only use prayer as a strategy against the enemy but fasting as well. When we fast our focus shifts from what we want and desire to what God wants and desires and that shift change can be one of the most powerful, defining moments in your walk with Christ!

"Therefore we do not give up. Even though our outer person is being destroyed, our inner person is being renewed day by day. For our momentary light affliction is producing for us an absolutely incomparable eternal weight of glory. So we do not focus on what is seen but on what is unseen. For what is seen is temporary, but what is unseen is eternal."
2 Corinthians 4:16-18 HCSB

We may often find ourselves in moments where it is hard to remain focused on God's promises, and the mission we have all been called to as believers in Christ.

As I read the above scriptures I thought of Noah and how he must have felt. He knew the promises God had made to him, he also knew the mission. And while so many around him could have possibly chosen to make a mockery of him, he never lost focus of what God had commanded of him. Now, the Bible doesn't tell us about the reaction of the people while Noah built the ark but imagine what would it be like if a modern-day Noah was told to build an ark for God. Media outlets would have a field day! He would be talked about, giggled at, and probably by many of us who profess to be believers and followers of Jesus Christ.

Focus.
The center of activity.
To pay particular attention to.

When our everyday lives are filled with calendars and schedules, work and school, spouses and children, it can be difficult to not be distracted and to not lose our focus on what God is asking of us; what He has called each of us to do.

It's easy to let the day pass by without reading our bibles. It's easy to say, "I'll catch up on my devotions tomorrow." It's easy for us to 'put off' God.

There's a saying, "Out of Sight, Out of Mind"
It's true in many situations. But it shouldn't be true in this scenario.

God wants to see your mind focused. Focused on Him. On praising Him, on worshipping Him, on praying and speaking to Him.

Not Him being last on your to do list, distracted by people's opinions, your family, your career or even your ministry. He needs and desires for you to have alone time, intimate one on one time with Him.

Don't let the world around you and the afflictions you face distract you from the mission God has called you to!

What we see is temporary. What God sees is eternal. Focus and fight accordingly!

Romans 12:12 says to be joyful in hope, patient in affliction and persistent in prayer.

As we are tested, trialed, and facing battles it's often hard to remember the importance of "patient in affliction".

The definition of affliction is something that causes pain or suffering. Words associated with affliction are distressed, torment, misery.

Thinking about times of affliction in my own life, it makes me cring at the thought of being patient in them as well.

Exactly how can one be patient when the world seems to be cavin in, when others appear to be stacked against you, when you are fightin one battle after another?

Our normal response is to fix the problem, to find a solution, a wa out. We want to claw our way to safety! We sometimes begin to buil walls of defense around our lives and our hearts. We search for th cure. We desperately seek for better than this moment. We mak decisions based on feelings and emotions rather than on the guidanc of the Holy Spirit. We want to attack, defend, guard and protec ourselves from the sting of rejection, loneliness, betrayal, hurt, an pain.

I'm reminded of Job in these trying times. The suffering he endure was unfathomable. He lost, and then lost more, and then lost even mor

I can't imagine the pain and the suffering! Pure Anguish! Then in hi deepest, most painful moment his friends wrongfully accuse him an stand against him!

"My friends scoff at me as I weep before God."
Job 16:20

Being patient in affliction has to be one of the hardest, seemingl unbearable trials we know, but through this endurance is built.

Endurance is the ability to withstand wear and tear, or the capacit in which one handles a situation without giving up.

"For this very reason, make every effort to supplement your faith wit goodness, goodness with knowledge, knowledge with self-control, sel control with endurance, endurance with godliness, godliness wit brotherly affection, and brotherly affection with love. For if thes qualities are yours and are increasing, they will keep you from bein useless or unfruitful in the knowledge of our Lord Jesus Christ."
2 Peter 1:5-8

"Consider it a great joy, my brothers, whenever you experience various trials, knowing that the testing of your faith produces endurance."
James 1:2-3

The building up of endurance can only happen by being stretched and pushed to our limits over and over. Each time our limit is stretched it reaches a new level. With each new level our endurance grows. As our endurance grows we become stronger, more prepared for the next punch.

Think of it this way, consider your job. We can use any job; being a mom, a hair stylist, a CEO, a doctor, a teacher. Put your "job" in the blank here.

When you began you were not at the same level you are now. You had to learn by schooling or experiences. You have been tested, failed, grown, and stretched to your limits and because of those moments you can now call yourself professional, experienced, mature, or recognized in your field.

Through patience during our afflictions, we gain endurance, and endurance allows us to overcome more than we thought possible.

If you are in a season of affliction, embrace it with patience, knowing your endurance will be built, you will be stronger, and you will overcome! Because He who is in you is greater than He who is in the world!

"You are from God, little children, and you have conquered them, because the One who is in you is greater than the one who is in the world."
1 John 4:4

This brings us to the purpose of our last and final strategy, fasting!

There are many occasions were fasting is mentioned in the bible, but today, I believe it is one of the most powerful tools, strategies and weapons we have that the enemy does not, yet it is the one that seems most of the world has allowed to collect dust and never be used.

Biblical fasting isn't only about being deprived of food and starving. It is the process of giving up your earthly desire, food, for a spiritual purpose.

One of the most often used examples of fasting is in the book of Daniel, chapter 1. This is known as the Daniel fast even in today's modern medicine world. So, what makes this particular fast so important?

Let's look at the scriptures and examine the purpose of Daniel fasting.

"Daniel determined that he would not defile himself with the king's food or with the wine he drank. So he asked permission from the chief official not to defile himself. God had granted Daniel favor and compassion from the chief official, yet he said to Daniel, "My lord the king assigned your food and drink. I'm afraid of what would happen if he saw your faces looking thinner than those of the other young men your age. You would endanger my life with the king." So Daniel said to the guard whom the chief official had assigned to Daniel, Hananiah, Mishael, and Azariah, "Please test your servants for 10 days. Let us be given vegetables to eat and water to drink. Then examine our appearance and the appearance of the young men who are eating the king's food, and deal with your servants based on what you see." He agreed with them about this and tested them for 10 days. At the end of 10 days they looked better and healthier than all the young men who were eating the king's food. So the guard continued to remove their food and the wine they were to drink and gave them vegetables."
Daniel 1:8-16

In the beginning of the book of Daniel we learn that the Lord had handed King Jehoiakim, of Judah, over to King Nebuchadnezzar, of Babylon. The king orders some of the Israelite's young men be brought in to learn the ways of the Chaldeans, their language and their literature, in order to become servants in the king's court.

Among these men chosen were, Daniel, Hananiah, Mishael, and Azariah. In an effort to have them honor the false gods of Babylon, the king changes their names to Belteshazzar, Shadrach, Meshach, and Abednego. Their birth given names honored the God of Israel, but their new names had meanings that only honored false gods. These men were also to eat food and drink wine from the king. Now, at first this doesn't sound like a big deal. After all, when we read stories of a king's palace in fairytales, we often see a table set for a king with almost any food imaginable. That seems more like an honor rather than a punishment. However, we have to look at the full scenario. These were Israelites who by law had to refrain from eating certain foods. The wine they were offered was also used as drink offerings to the false gods of Babylon. Therefore, if Daniel had chosen to simple remain silent and do as he was told, he would have dishonored God. Rather than sit quietly, Daniel spoke up and requested only vegetables and water for 10 days, challenging the guard to compare the four of them to the remaining who would be partaking in the king's food. At the end of the 10 days, the four Israelites were stronger and healthier in appearance. So they were allowed to continue with this fast, guaranteeing they didn't have to dishonor God. In verses 17-21, we find out that God blessed them with knowledge, understanding, and wisdom. They were 10 times better than all other servants in the king's court.

Daniel chose to honor God through fasting and was rewarded with greater wisdom because of that. Our first lesson of fasting is this, when we fast for the purpose of remaining honorable to God, He will be faithful to provide what we need. Daniel was shown favor by God for honoring Him.

"For you were bought with a price, So glorify God in your body."
1 Corinthians 6:20 ESV

There is an even greater lesson within this chapter as well. Daniel honored God because he loved God, not because he thought he deserved a reward. Our hearts have much to do with our fasting outcome. We can not give of ourselves merely expecting something in return. We must fast with a heart conditioned and ready to honor and serve our Lord, whether we are given blessings and favor, or we aren't

"Whenever you fast, don't be sad-faced like the hypocrites. For they make their faces unattractive, so their fasting is obvious to people. I assure you: They've got their reward! But when you fast, put oil on your head, and wash your face, so that you don't show your fasting to people but to your Father who is in secret. And your Father who sees in secret will reward you.
Matthew 6:16-18

Finally, the third lesson we can learn from Daniel in fasting is that he was prepared. His mind was set to serve and honor God no matter what happened. He made up his mind not to defile himself and not to give in to the pressures around him. We, too, must be prepared as we begin to use this battle strategy.

"Therefore, if anyone cleanses himself from what is dishonorable, he will be a vessel for honorable use, set apart as holy, useful to the master of the house, ready for every good work."
2 Timothy 2:21

Fasting allows us to align with what God desires from us, in order to completely fulfill His purpose for us and for His kingdom. When you sacrifice, from a place of honor and worship, you will begin to experience a shifting in your life that is indescribable.

Jesus gave His authority and power to the disciples to heal the sick and cast out demons. But there is one particular situation that happen with the disciples that teaches us the importance of fighting our battle with all available strategies and weapons.
In Matthew 17, Mark 9, and Luke 9, we read about a father who ha brought his only son to Jesus to be healed from demon possession. Thi

particular demon is causing disaster and damage in many ways. The boy's body begins to convulse, he foams at the mouth, he shrieks and wounds himself, grinds his teeth, his body stiffens, he is unable to speak, and it causes him to fall into fire and into water in attempts to destroy him. While Jesus was on the mountain with Peter, James, and John (sons of Zebedee), this father had brought his son to the remaining disciples for help. They attempted to cast out the demon from him but were unsuccessful. When Jesus arrives, the scribes are disputing the disciples. The crowd notices Jesus and runs to Him. Can you imagine the chaos that is happening in this place?

They bring the boy to Jesus and immediately the demon recognizes Him and the boy begins to convulse and is thrown to the ground. Then Jesus rebukes the mute and deaf spirit and commands for it to come out of the boy. It comes out of the boy and he is healed, once and for all.

Once the disciples and Jesus are alone again in private, they ask Him why they were unable to cast this demon out.

Then Jesus says to them:

"However, this kind does not come out except by prayer and fasting"
Matthew 17:21

This scripture, or at least the ending that we are focused on, fasting, is often debated on whether or not it was included in the original content of scriptures. It is even completely removed from some translations. However, we know that all God's word is truth and I firmly believe that if God had intended something to be left out, then it would have never made it into the bible in the first place.

Another point I want to briefly touch on is found in Mark 2. Jesus is questioned as to why the disciples of John the Baptist, and the pharisees fast, but yet His disciples do not. Jesus explained to them His disciples did not need to fast, because He was with them. Perhaps this is why the disciples were unable to cast out this demon. I'm not a biblical scholar by any means, however, I do know this truth; if fasting was good enough for Jesus then it is surely good enough for me.

"A disciple is not above his teacher, but everyone who is fully trained will be like his teacher."
Luke 6:40 HCSB

Jesus fasted for 40 days and nights in the wilderness. He didn't have to fast, but He knew there was spiritual wisdom to be unlocked through the giving up of fleshly, physical needs and relying on God to supply food to the body for spiritual needs.

Fasting can open your eyes to a whole new perspective. When you fully focus on God and His infinite power, rather than relying on your human observation, your views of the world around you begin to change.

Human eyes see loss where God's eyes see a ram in the thicket.

Human eyes see a giant where God's eyes see promise.

Human eyes see a battle where God's eyes see victory.

In the times I have fasted, I have seen God's power in my life more prominent than at any other time. My relationship with the Lord has increased in intimacy during these times and I have seen an outpouring of truth that fasting allows me to be 100% prepared for battle!

Now it's your turn!

Your battles must be prepared for, your armor must be put on, and you must know that we have victory in Jesus Christ.

John 19:30 tells us the very words we should feel obligated to remember, *'He said, "It is finished!"'*

This is our hope as we prepare and as we battle.

This is our hope and our proof that we will have victory because of Christ!

Sister, you aren't fighting against the person, the situation, or the circumstance! Your fight is against the enemy! Don't let him deceive you!

Rise up!
Warrior woman, it is time to fight!
It's time for war!
Gather your armor!
Prepare for battle
And for victory!

Battle Plan #10
FAST

You need to study fasting on your own. Search diligently in prayer for how, when, how long, what foods and all the questions you probably are now asking yourself about fasting. There are plenty more scriptures about fasting that I didn't mention. Find them and study!

When you conquer this battle, get a clean fresh notebook, because the enemy will begin another, and you will start your preparation all over at Chapter 1.

Each time your battle, endurance is built.

You are strong!

We Are Giant Slaying

Light Shining

Mountain Moving

Praise Singing

Sword Swinging

Jesus Loving

Warrior Women!

Contact Information

To book Andrea Kellum as a guest speaker for your next women's event, please email:

info@andreakellum.com

To join the Coffee and Jesus devotion group on facebook go to:

https://www.facebook.com/groups/166846717211514/

For more information on other available books, devotions, and Women's bible studies by Andrea Kellum please visit:

www.andreakellum.com

Mailing Address:

Andrea Kellum

Changing Crowns Ministries

P.O. Box 314

Woodstock, Alabama 35188

Follow on Social Media:

Facebook: www.facebook.com/changingcrownsministries

Instagram: www.instagram.com/andrea_kellum

Made in the USA
San Bernardino,
CA

56932831R00076